THE PENDERGAST MACHINE

THE URBAN LIFE IN AMERICA SERIES

RICHARD C. WADE, GENERAL EDITOR

STANLEY BUDER
PULLMAN: An Experiment in Industrial Order
and Community Planning 1880–1930

ALLEN F. DAVIS
SPEARHEADS FOR REFORM: The Social Settlements
and the Progressive Movement 1890–1914

KENNETH T. JACKSON
THE KU KLUX KLAN IN THE CITY, 1915–1930

LYLE W. DORSETT
THE PENDERGAST MACHINE

THE PENDERGAST
MACHINE

LYLE W. DORSETT

NEW YORK
OXFORD UNIVERSITY PRESS
1968

To my parents and my wife

Foreword

The city boss and the urban machine comprise a unique element of our political system, and they have played a dominant role in urban politics for almost a century. The rise of the modern city saw the rise of the political machine. Though under continuous attack from the "best" people, machines and their leaders in every section of the country managed to accumulate power and the control of local government. In the process, they put their particular stamp on city halls and county court houses, and gave the public life of the metropolis a flavor and texture theretofore unknown. Whether the machine is now dead or merely transformed to adjust to new conditions, is perhaps an open question. But it is certain that the system in its classical sense has disappeared, leaving behind only a few faint echoes of the great hurrahs of an earlier time.

Despite the importance of the machine, there have been few serious attempts to see its development within the context of the urban explosion of the late nineteenth century and early twentieth century. Most early scholarly analyses emphasized the corruption and venality which accompanied machine rule; more recent scholarship has tended to minimize the boss's questionable means and to call attention to substantive achievements. But no one has written a detailed account of the origins of an urban machine, traced its growth and transformation, and explained its decline and disappearance.

In this volume, Lyle Dorsett begins to fill that need. And the choice of the Pendergast machine for study is a particularly happy one. It was a machine built on the classical model; it achieved an extraordinary dominance in Kansas City politics; at its height its influence encompassed the state house and reached into the New Deal in Washington. In its waning days it was also monumentally corrupt. And as an unexpected dividend of the story, a cog in that Kansas City machine in the heydey of boss rule would one day emerge as future President Harry S Truman—untouched by the machine's sordid practices yet a beneficiary of its power.

Mr. Dorsett's concern, however, is not to make judgments on the Pendergast machine, but to seek its origins, to see what stratagems and conditions explain its growth, and later to find out what brought down the most spectacularly successful boss in the nation. The story covers five decades. It begins with Jim Pendergast, a newcomer to Kansas City, who put together a political organization out of the polyglot, low-income population of the West Bottoms. The operation looked modest enough at the outset; it covered only a single ward and sent Pendergast to the city council. Yet the level of control was unusual, and the First Ward, by its ability to throw large majorities one way or the other, quickly achieved disproportionate power in the city.

Soon Jim Pendergast would add the equally motley North End to his domain, thus solidifying his "Goat" faction in the Democratic party against the rival faction, Shannon's "Rabbits," and also widening his influence in the city. The first years of the machine were not very gentle, but they were, on the whole, honest. To be sure the boss's income came from saloons and, to some degree, from gambling and prostitution, but the votes were seldom fraudulent, and no one doubted the genuine popularity of Jim Pendergast in his own neighborhood. Nor was Jim above supporting improvements, even if the benefits to the downtown wards were not readily apparent.

The Pendergast machine, however, was developed against the changing canvas of a dynamic city. If it was to survive, it would have to change with the town. In 1910, after Jim Pendergast was too ill to go on, his brother Tom picked up the reins. He quickly spread the operation into the burgeoning residential wards and forged alliances with various elements of the business community. What had once been the political expression of depressed areas in the city had now become a massive county-wide operation.

But success would soon spoil Tom Pendergast. When he moved out to a $150,000 mansion away from the constituents that had given the machine its start, he tore up his roots. He joined the fashionable set, vacationed abroad, and was flattered by the press. He even managed not only to support a charter "reform" movement but to turn it to his own advantage. Money and power came easily. He picked up $750,000 on one transaction; he was making and breaking governors and senators. When the New Deal came into being in Washington, no one was more powerful in Missouri than Tom Pendergast, and favors and attention flowed to the Kansas City boss.

Yet within a few years the whole edifice collapsed. The end did not come because the New Deal's welfare programs took away the machine's source of power, for it was too soon for that. It came with scandals connected with the 1936 election. Ironically, the outcome of the election was never in doubt, and the wide-scale fraud was unnecessary as well as foolish. Within months, the man who wielded unprecedented power in the city and state was in jail; soon he was dead. Mr. Dorsett tells the story with detachment

and understanding. Though its setting was Kansas City, it occurred
in scores of cities elsewhere; though it happened between 1890
and 1940, its relevance is almost timeless.

RICHARD C. WADE

GENERAL EDITOR

URBAN LIFE IN AMERICA SERIES

Chicago, Ill.
November 1967

Preface

A few years ago historian Eric L. McKitrick urged students of American politics to take another look at political machines. He argued that an interest in reform had stimulated most of the previous studies on the subject, and that it was now time to examine dispassionately the structural and functional side of machine politics.[1] The present study is an attempt to examine the Pendergast machine in that light. In the following pages I have tried to answer such questions as, What is a political machine? How does it function? Where is the source of its power? What does it do with its power? How does it meet the challenges that it faces?

The roots of the Pendergast machine go back to the 1880's when James Pendergast became active in Kansas City's extremely disorganized political milieu. Neither Republicans nor Democrats had a permanent political organization in the growing western Missouri city. A saloonkeeper in the industrial river bottoms district, the

elder Pendergast gradually replaced political chaos with order by
creating the city's first permanent Democratic club. He became a
ward boss in the classical tradition by providing welfare services
to his underprivileged Negro, Italian, and Irish constituents. At the
same time he tutored his younger brother, Thomas Joseph Pendergast, in the art of politics.

When the founder of the Pendergast machine died in 1911, his
brother inherited the organization. He expanded the river ward
organization until it encompassed the entire city, and rural Jackson
County. As the machine grew, it became increasingly complex. This
was necessarily the case because Kansas City was primarily a mercantile and financial center with a large, native-born, middle-class
population. In fact, foreign-born voters never numbered much over
6 per cent of the population. Thus anyone who hoped to create a
city- and county-wide organization would have to do much more
than provide for the underprivileged.

Tom Pendergast met the challenge, and achieved power by providing services for the diverse interests in his community. He
always cared for the underprivileged, but he did much more.
Middle-class citizens in residential districts were served, as were
individuals in the professions and the business community. Always
a realist, he summed up his own success: "People work for a party
because they can get a job or get a favor—special privilege gets
the votes." [2]

This study encompasses the life cycle of the Pendergast machine
from its earliest beginnings to its inglorious fall. Each of the chap-
ters covers a stage in the organization's growth by demonstrating
how the Pendergasts continually searched for ways to serve, and
find areas of agreement among, the numerous individuals and
groups that had interests to protect and goals to attain. The em-
phasis is on the successive steps of expansion from the control of
a single ward to eventual domination of the whole city. And finally
I show how the political leaders of Kansas City, once they had
organized their community, were able to extend the range of their
influence throughout the entire state.

The first part of this book grew out of a University of Kansas City master's thesis on James Pendergast. I am deeply indebted to A. Theodore Brown at the University of Wisconsin at Milwaukee, who first suggested the topic of James Pendergast to me. Professor Brown was at that time the Director of the History of Kansas City Research Project. He provided a research assistantship for two years which enabled me to prepare the thesis. Much more important, though, was his perceptive and patient guidance, which I greatly appreciate.

Professor Richard S. Kirkendall at the University of Missouri at Columbia encouraged me to expand the earlier study into a doctoral dissertation on the Pendergast machine. He directed the dissertation, discovered source materials for me, and contributed many invaluable ideas. I am also indebted to him for the enduring inspiration that he has given me through his energetic devotion to the historian's craft.

My gratitude also goes to Allen F. Davis for reading the entire manuscript and offering many suggestions for improvement. Two friends, Richard O. Davies and Franklin D. Mitchell, offered helpful advice. Richard C. Wade, the general editor of the series, and Sheldon Meyer of Oxford University Press, offered criticisms that certainly improved the manuscript. Many others also provided assistance. Mrs. Nancy Prewitt and her staff at the Western Historical Manuscripts Division of the University of Missouri continually went out of their way to aid me. Miss Katherine Goldsmith at the Missouri Valley Room of the Kansas City, Missouri Public Library spent hours locating useful materials. Miss Elizabeth Drewry and the staff at the Franklin D. Roosevelt Library were extremely helpful, as was Dr. Philip C. Brooks at the Harry S Truman Library.

I wish to thank the following editors for granting permission to use portions of articles published in their journals: Harwood Hinton, *Arizona and the West*, Mrs. Dana O. Jensen, *Bulletin of the Missouri Historical Society*, and Stuart Levine, *Midcontinent American Studies Journal*.

Finally, the late James M. Pendergast, nephew of the Pendergast brothers, deserves special mention. Each time that I called upon him to answer questions and share his experiences he did so happily and with candor.

L. W. D.

Los Angeles, California
November 1967

Contents

THE PENDERGAST MACHINE

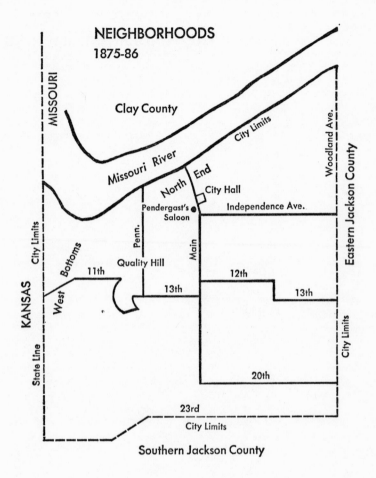

NEIGHBORHOODS
1875-86

Clay County

Missouri River

MISSOURI

City Limits

North End

City Hall

Pendergast's Saloon

Independence Ave.

Penn.

Woodland Ave.

Eastern Jackson County

KANSAS

City Limits

West Bottoms

11th

Quality Hill

Main

13th

12th

13th

City Limits

20th

State Line

23rd

City Limits

Southern Jackson County

1

The Roots of Political Control

James Pendergast was born in the little town of Gallipolis, Ohio, on the banks of the Ohio River, on January 27, 1856. When he was two years old, his Irish parents packed him up with the rest of the family possessions and moved to St. Joseph, Missouri. The second of nine children, Jim Pendergast attended the public schools in St. Joseph. After his twentieth birthday, he left St. Joseph and went to Kansas City, where the opportunities for a young man were much greater.

Pendergast arrived in Kansas City in 1876 with only a few dollars in his pocket. An intense, ambitious young man, he was willing to accept any kind of work. He rented a room in the West Bottoms, and immediately found employment in the packing houses. Physically, Pendergast was well-suited for heavy work. Although not even five feet nine inches tall, he was the picture of strength with his short, thick neck and massive shoulders and arms. But he did not like packing-house work. After a few weeks he took a job as a puddler in an iron foundry.

The life of a puddler did not fulfill Pendergast's ambitions any more than packing-house work had. Thus in 1881, after a horse

named Climax paid well at the racetrack, he quit his job and
purchased a combination hotel and saloon with his winnings. The
Climax, as he named his saloon, was located on St. Louis Avenue
in the heart of Kansas City's industrial West Bottoms.[1]

By 1891 Pendergast had become a successful businessman. He
soon was able to sell his original saloon and purchase a new one
in the same neighborhood. He kept the hotel and he also bought
a second saloon in the North End. Pendergast's saloon-keeping
career would prove to be extremely advantageous once he became
active in local politics.

Kansas City was a spectacle of immense diversity during the three
and a half decades that Pendergast pursued his business and political fortunes there. A year before he opened his saloon, the
United States Census showed the population of Kansas City to be
55,785. By 1910, just prior to his death, the population had soared
to over 248,000. This growing population, composed of both Negro
and white native-born Americans as well as German, Irish, Italian,
and other foreign-born persons, spread over the city, which was
made up of neighborhoods no less diverse than the groups which
inhabited them.

The West Bottoms, the neighborhood Jim Pendergast represented in the city council for eighteen years, was bounded on the
west by the state line, on the north by the river and railroad tracks,
and on the east by exclusive Quality Hill. It encompassed packing
houses, railroad yards, machine shops, factories, and warehouses.
In many respects this neighborhood changed very little during the
years that Pendergast lived there. When he came to the West Bottoms in 1876 it was the heart of the city's industrial district, and it
remained so until after his death. Likewise, before he came to
Kansas City, the West Bottoms had poor streets, many of which
were unpaved or in need of repair. Three decades later mud and
dust still covered most of the neighborhood's thoroughfares.

The West Bottom's population, which was composed mostly of
low-income Negroes living in the eastern part of the neighborhood,
and Irish, German, and native laborers in the remaining portions,

did not change its character to any noticeable extent while the neighborhood was Pendergast's political domain. The ubiquitous junk shops and second-hand stores on Ninth Street were patronized by these low-income laborers, most of whom lived in overcrowded tenements and shanties. The perennial problem of open sewers and gutters, coupled with overcrowded living conditions, constantly threatened the inhabitants with disease and added to the unpleasantness of their surroundings.

Immediately adjacent to the West Bottoms on the northeast was the neighborhood known as the North End. In his early political career, "Big Jim," as Pendergast's friends called him, extended his political strength from its matrix in the West Bottoms to every corner of the North End. That neighborhood was not nearly so industrialized as the West Bottoms, but in many other respects the two areas were very similar. The North End did not have as large a Negro population as the West Bottoms, but it was largely inhabited by poor laborers, who lived in dilapidated tenement houses. Most of the city's Italian citizens were housed there in a district commonly referred to as "Little Italy."

Most of the area provided nothing better than crowded tenement housing for its inhabitants. A local newspaper writer, appalled by the living conditions, reported that

> for whole blocks of inhabited buildings there are no yards. Tired mothers sit on doorsteps with fretful babies in their arms and children swarm over the streets, dodging electric cars and other vehicles.[2]

The "dingy North End," as it was sometimes called, was lined with old buildings used for small factories and tenements. Most of these four- and five-story buildings were decrepit firetraps, which would have collapsed immediately in the event of a fire. It was here that the city's "red light" districts flourished, and where most of the local underworld activities were born.

Overlooking both the North End and the West Bottoms was the neighborhood called Quality Hill. During the Civil War era this

neighborhood on the highest peak of the city's west bluffs began
to be settled by Kansas City's elite. By the time Jim Pendergast
came to Kansas City in the 1870's, Quality Hill was illuminated by
gas streetlights, while much of the West Bottoms and North
End remained in darkness. The glow of these lights displayed the
pretentious brick houses that decorated Quality Hill, as well as
the luxurious hotel called the Coates House, complete with marble
swimming pool and copper-roofed towers. But the passing years
brought marked changes to Quality Hill. The wealthy social elite
gradually moved to the southern and eastern portions of the growing city to make room for the expanding commercial interests. By
1890 business houses dotted many parts of Quality Hill, and the
best residential districts were to be found to the east and south.[3]

These diverse neighborhoods, with their motley populations,
made up the Kansas City in which Jim Pendergast became a political success. When Pendergast first came to Kansas City in 1876,
city politics reflected more chaos than organization. Between 1870
and 1889, none of the wards or neighborhoods showed any political
stability. The election returns reported in the newspapers for those
two decades show that neither the Democratic nor Republican
parties had a consistent majority in any ward or neighborhood.
There were many reasons for this, but a marked lack of political
leadership and organization played a significant role. The Democratic party, for example, had no permanent Democratic club or
organization until 1890, and the Republican party was so dis-
membered by factional strife that it could seldom work efficiently.
Also, neither party had for any period of time, other than immediately prior to an election, more than one or two men who devoted
much time to city politics. Party leaders came and went with the
annual city elections because many of them were businessmen with
only an incidental interest in local politics.

While Kansas City politics lacked the organization of Boss
Tweed's New York and Abraham Ruef's San Francisco, it did not
lack the color. The city elections which were held each April were
often preceded by gala events. A torchlight procession around the

city's market square, a brass band playing, and men carrying pictures of the candidates or large signs bearing such mottos as "No Man Owns the Irish Vote" and "We Are Opposed to Rings and Cliques" were by no means unusual. Pre-election rallies were sometimes introduced by cornet music, and crowds would gather in the streets to hear five or six speakers praise their candidates.

Jim Pendergast took his first active interest in Kansas City politics in 1884. In March of that year, prior to the city election, Pendergast attended the Democratic primary in the West Bottoms' Sixth Ward. The "Bloody Sixth," as the ward was tagged because of the many fights there on election day, held its primaries in the same manner that the other five wards did. "Mob" primaries, as those meetings were called, were merely assemblages of the party's voters who met en masse and voted on delegates to represent them in the party's city convention. Jim Pendergast was one of the eleven delegates elected by the Democrats in the "Bloody Sixth" to represent them in the 1884 Democratic City Convention.

For the next two years, the West Bottoms saloonkeeper was not active in either the primaries or the city convention. Then in 1887 he was selected again to represent the West Bottoms in the city convention. By this time, Pendergast was representing the First Ward. A change in the ward boundaries in 1886 had altered the old "Bloody Sixth" so that it included virtually all of the West Bottoms, and it was renamed the First Ward.

In 1888 the First Ward became more centralized, when the Democratic leaders decided that voters should elect a chairman of the meeting instead of participating in the old "mob" primaries. The chairman would then appoint a committee which would handpick the delegates to the city convention. By rallying a simple majority to the lightly attended primary, a faction leader could get himself or one of his men elected chairman. By controlling the chair, a faction could control the delegates and have a solid block of votes for any of the candidates it might wish to support in the city convention.[4]

This change in the method of selecting delegates was not unique

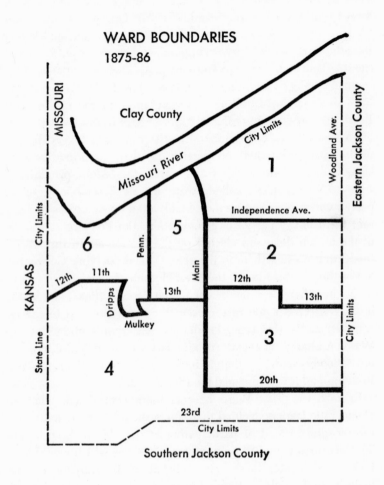

WARD BOUNDARIES
1875-86

Clay County

MISSOURI

Missouri River

Clay County

City Limits

1

Woodland Ave.

Eastern Jackson County

City Limits

6

Penn.

5

Independence Ave.

2

Main

12th

11th

12th

13th

Dripps

13th

Mulkey

City Limits

KANSAS

State Line

4

3

20th

23rd
City Limits

Southern Jackson County

to the First Ward. It in fact had been going on in the Democratic primaries in several other wards since 1885. Just how much influence Jim Pendergast had in making this change is impossible to say, although in 1888 he was selected to be on the committee which chose the delegates and again in 1889.

Pendergast was by no means the commander of the First Ward Democracy at this time. Two First Ward faction leaders, Edward Kelly and John Grady, were competing for leadership. Since the mid-'eighties these two Irishmen had been struggling for control of the primaries, but they usually agreed to a compromise. On two occasions, however, they failed to compromise and competed in the primaries. The struggles resulted in the election of two groups of delegates one time, and a deadlocked primary which was forced to adjourn the other. It was on those two occasions, 1886 and 1890, that the astute Pendergast took no part in the First Ward primaries.

Neither Kelly nor Grady ever managed to direct the Democratic politics of the First Ward. That was to be reserved for Jim Pendergast. All the time that Kelly, the First Ward member of the Democratic City Executive Committee, and Grady, the twice-elected councilman from the First Ward, fought for control, Pendergast refused to take sides. He co-operated with both men. In 1890 he opened the doors of his hotel, Pendergast Hall, to Kelly so that he could hold a campaign meeting for First Ward Democrats. Pendergast had gained the favor of Grady, too, for in March 1892 the latter made known his wish to retire from the council, if Jim Pendergast could replace him.

Pendergast's refusal to take sides in the First Ward faction troubles paid rich dividends. By 1892 he was the undisputed leader of the First Ward Democracy. For the first time in years the *Kansas City Star*, an independent local newspaper, could report that a Democrat had "a walk away for the [alderman] nomination" in the First Ward.[5]

The nominee for the First Ward's seat in the lower house of the city council had more than just party support; he had the support of the citizens in the West Bottoms. A First Ward political rally

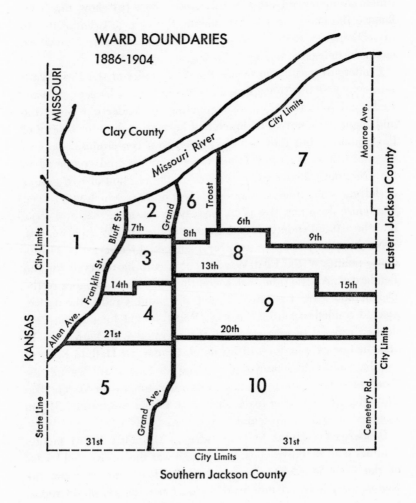

WARD BOUNDARIES
1886-1904

MISSOURI

Clay County

Missouri River

City Limits

Monroe Ave.

Eastern Jackson County

KANSAS

City Limits

State Line

Bluff St.

Franklin St.

Allen Ave.

7th

Grand

1

2

3

14th

4

21st

Grand Ave.

5

31st

8th

Troost

6

6th

8

13th

7

9th

15th

9

20th

Cemetery Rd.

City Limits

10

31st

City Limits

Southern Jackson County

just prior to the city election demonstrated "Big Jim's" popularity.
A local newspaper reported that the meeting on Genesee Street, in
the West Bottoms, was attended by

> the hard handed men of the First Ward . . . in oily blue jump-
> ers, . . . with packing house mud on their boots, switchmen,
> freight handlers, engineers. Lots of them, too. There were not
> many silk hats in the crowd. . . .⁶

One speaker, after complimenting the First Ward Democrats for
nominating Pendergast, continued by saying:

> there is no kinder hearted or more sympathetic man in Kansas
> City than Jim Pendergast. He will go down in his pockets after
> his last cent to help a friend. No man is more easily moved to
> sympathy or good sense than Jim Pendergast.⁷

When the speech was finished, the laboring-men's applause produced "a prodigious noise" and then Pendergast entered. "Terrific
yells" ensued, and the saloonkeeper responded by saying, "I never
attempted a speech in all my life, but if you elect me I will do my
duty." ⁸

The election returns confirmed all reports of Jim Pendergast's
popularity. He defeated his Republican opponent by a five-to-one
majority. From April 1892 until April 1910 "Alderman Jim" would
direct First Ward politics. The West Bottoms would no longer be
without consistency in its political behavior, nor would it be split
by factional strife. The political situation had changed. Pendergast,
according to the *Kansas City Star*, was to be "King of the First."

In April 1892 Jim Pendergast took his seat in the lower house of
Kansas City's Common Council. The Charter of 1889 had created a
bicameral legislature for Kansas City, consisting of an upper and
lower house with each containing as many members as there were
wards. Members of the upper house were elected at large for a
period of four years, while members of the lower house were elected
by the ward they represented for two years. Neither house wielded
more strength than the other, for ordinances of any type could

originate in either house, had to pass both houses before they could be sent to the mayor for approval, and required a two-thirds majority of both houses to survive the mayor's veto.[9]

During his initial year in the lower house, the inexperienced alderman did nothing to attract attention. He was ignored by the newspapers and scarcely known outside of the First Ward. But in his own neighborhood most people knew Jim Pendergast. He could not be overlooked when walking down the street. A man who loved to eat, by this time he weighed well over two hundred pounds. Overweight but obviously strong, "Big Jim" became famous for his black Bismarck mustache and his small bow tie.

After a year though, the politician from the West Bottoms became well known. William Rockhill Nelson, the reformist editor of the *Kansas City Star*, focused his attention on Pendergast. Baron Bill, as Nelson's enemies called him, believed that a municipal government should be run as "a business affair." [10] Using his newspaper to support and inaugurate many progressive projects in Kansas City, Nelson was first attracted to Alderman Pendergast because of his position on the appropriation of city funds for a garbage system. Pendergast according to the *Star*, said that "there is nothing that this city needs more than a garbage system," as he pledged his support for a $20,000 garbage fund.[11]

Alderman Jim also received early praise as a friend of progress when he took a bold stand in the lower house against a "wide open [telephone] franchise" which might well have pushed the telephone rates much higher than they were at that time. Even in the face of increased pressure from the Telephone Company to change his position, Pendergast remained adamant and the company was forced to compromise.[12]

The First Ward alderman distinguished himself as a fighter for the working-man as well. He urged the construction of a city park for the poor West Bottomites, and he led a battle to allow the city to go into debt if necessary rather than cut the salaries of the already underpaid firemen.

This issue over the firemen's salaries drew much attention. The

mayor and city comptroller had discovered that the fire department had overdrawn its budget for the year. The two officials,
therefore, asked the council to cut firemen's salaries by 15 per cent.
The mayor and comptroller were Democrats, but they met strong
opposition from four aldermen within their own party.

The city hall was located in the North End, and on the night
that the salary issue was taken up in the council, a crowd of laborers gathered outdoors. The upper house voted to cut the firemen's
salaries. When the news reached the gathering outdoors, a chorus
of hooting and yelling began. The crowd challenged the upper
house to send the ordinance to the lower house, where four friends
of the low-income working-men resided. The ordinance was de-
tained several days, but when it did go to the lower house, the two
North End aldermen, Martin Regan of the Sixth Ward, and Andy
Foley of the Second, joined forces with Pendergast and his friend
John Fitzpatrick from an adjoining neighborhood. The "Big Four"
as the *Star* called them, buried the bill so deep that it was never
resurrected.[13]

A few months later Pendergast again supported his constituents
by working against a proposal to move the only fire station in the
West Bottoms to Quality Hill. Again Alderman Jim allied himself
with Regan and Foley, and the three men were able to win
enough support to block the move.

Pendergast's stand in the council undoubtedly produced a vote
or two of confidence for him. The big saloonkeeper, however, did
as much work outside the council to increase his following during
his first term in office as he did from within. When a dozen men
were arrested for working bunco games (betting swindles) at the
race track, Alderman Jim put up bond in the police court for
several of them. Although running to help a man arrested for
working a bunco game would have been looked upon with disdain by the voters on Quality Hill, the laborers in the West Bottoms were more convinced than ever that Jim was their friend.

One did not have to be in trouble to get help from the First
Ward Irishman, because every month Pendergast was a bank

teller for many of the railroad and packing-house workers in the
West Bottoms. Cash was scarce in those days, so Jim kept the
safe in his saloon full of paper and silver on payday in order to
cash the checks of the working-men. "They spent some of it
across the bar," asserted William Reddig, who knew personally
some of Alderman Jim's close friends,

> but Jim did not make that a requisite. Men learned that he had
> an interest in humanity outside of business and that he could be
> trusted, and they returned the favor by patronizing his saloon
> and giving him their confidence.[14]

During his first term in the lower house, Pendergast had done
much both in and out of the city council to increase his popularity
with the First Ward voters. In other quarters though, he had made
enemies. William R. Nelson and his *Star* criticized the Irish saloonkeeper on occasion, especially when he fought the efforts to cut
firemen's salaries and move the fire station. The *Star* was not alone
in criticizing Pendergast and some of his fellow politicians. Kansas
City's bosses could sympathize with New York's "Big Tim" Sullivan
and Richard Croker, for they had their own counterpart of New
York's Reverend Charles Parkhurst to contend with. The Reverend
John Sewell, one of Kansas City's Congregational ministers, was an
ardent reformer in the style of Parkhurst. Attempting to reform the
city government as well as souls, Sewell hoped to purge Kansas
City of all "professional politicians . . . who emerge from tending
bar in some corner dram shop, [and] begin to rapidly climb the
ladder of political influence." [15]

Kansas Citians did not have to look far to find the men to whom
Sewell was referring. Only three city politicians who had gained
prominence in the past two years were saloonkeepers, and all three,
Pendergast, Regan, and Foley, represented the wards of West
Bottoms and North End. However, opposition to Jim Pendergast
was ineffective in the face of all that he had been doing for his
West Bottoms neighbors. When he decided to run for alderman
again in the spring of 1894, his popularity, which he had enhanced

by his actions in the council, from behind the bar of his saloon, and by the little personal favors that he performed, was confirmed by his re-election.

The significance of Pendergast's re-election in 1894 can only be appreciated when one views the opposition he faced. The strongest opposition, according to the Democratic *Kansas City Times*, was "a new factor" in local politics. It was the American Protective Association. According to the *Times*, the A.P.A. had "but one plank in its platform . . . opposition to Catholics." [16] The A.P.A. was strong in the Middle West at that time and had a sizable influence on Kansas City politics. The A.P.A. members managed to gain partial control of the Republican City Convention in 1894, and they succeeded in getting several of their candidates nominated, including Webster Davis, a candidate for mayor.

The Irish-Catholic Pendergast not only had the A.P.A.-dominated Republicans to face in the election of 1894, he also had a newly formed Independent ticket to fight. It was headed by a Democrat, Frank Cooper, a partner in the livestock firm of Offut, Elmore & Cooper. This nonpartisan ticket had well-known Republicans and Democrats on it, all of whom were calling for a municipal government run on business principles, not political influence. The independent *Kansas City Star* and the hitherto Democratic *Times* both threw their support to the infant movement. The city's other leading newspaper, the *Journal*, backed the Republican ticket as usual and did not even mention the A.P.A. issue.

The many-sided opposition to the straight Democratic ticket, and especially the anti-Catholic crusade of the A.P.A. Republicans, pushed Jim Pendergast into an alliance with another rising young Catholic politician, Joe Shannon. Having made his political debut about the same time that Pendergast had, Joe Shannon, with the help of his brother Frank, was trying to establish himself in the city's largest ward, the Ninth.[17]

Pendergast, Shannon, and some other regular Democrats put up a ticket with a labor leader, Frank Johnson, at the top. But the wave of support won by the A.P.A. was too strong, and only Pendergast's First Ward gave Johnson a majority of its votes. The Republicans gained twenty-three out of twenty-five city offices; not one of the Independents was elected; and only two Democrats, Pendergast and Regan, were victorious. Actually, Pendergast was barely threatened. He had received 687 votes, and the Republican nominee obtained only 212. The Independent candidate proved to be the weakest of the three, finishing with only 137 votes.

The election demonstrated beyond a doubt that Pendergast was the only Democratic ward leader in the city who could deliver the votes when the chips were down. Every other ward in the city but two, including Regan's Sixth Ward and Shannon's Ninth, gave a majority of its votes to Webster Davis, the A.P.A. Republican. Although Andy Foley's old bailiwick, the Second Ward, did not go to Davis, it fell to the Independent candidate, Frank Cooper. And while Martin Regan had been able to get himself elected in the Sixth, he could not carry the remainder of the Democratic ticket with him. Only Pendergast had produced majorities for himself and the ticket.

There had been some fraud in the city election of 1894, but not in Pendergast's ward. The Shannons, who could not swing the Ninth Ward either legally or illegally, were involved in some crooked voting practices.[18] Investigators never found any evidence of fraud in the First Ward while Pendergast resided there. With illegal voting practices being discovered in many other wards throughout the city during the years that Pendergast was a power in city politics, many people questioned the absence of fraud in the First. Alderman Jim had the answer. "I never needed a crooked vote. All I want is a chance for my friends to get to the polls."[19]

Although the First Ward Boss stole no votes, he did not consider the ordinances prohibiting gambling to be sacred—at least not during his early years as chief of the First Ward Democracy. By 1892, Jim had closed his saloon on St. Louis Avenue in the West Bottoms, but he retained the Pendergast Hotel. He had also opened a saloon in the North End's Second Ward, and another one in the West Bottoms' First Ward. There was gambling upstairs over both of these saloons during the summer of 1894. In August 1894, thirty-eight men were arrested in a big dice game in the North End saloon.[20]

As long as Thomas M. Speers remained the chief of police in Kansas City, gamblers were threatened. As early as April 1895 Marcy K. Brown, a faction leader in Jackson County politics, began pressuring Governor Stone to get rid of Speers. The control of the police was in the hands of the state at this time. The governor appointed a board of police commissioners for the city, and this board had the power to remove and appoint the chief of police and all of the patrolmen. The board also established the salaries of all members of the police force.

In late April 1895 Governor Stone appointed a new board of police commissioners. The new board soon dropped Speers as chief of police and replaced him with L. E. Irwin. Throughout the remainder of the year, the gambling games over both of Pendergast's saloons, which were operated by the notorious gambler Ed Findley, ran wide open without police interference.[21]

This situation caused the *Star* to begin a campaign against Chief Irwin and the "police-protected" games in the Alderman's saloons. There was increased pressure on Irwin from both the *Star* and a local reform organization, the Civic Federation, to close down the illegal games. The chief was forced into some token action. He made several raids on the Pendergast saloons, but the gamblers were usually tipped off by the police beforehand and had time to close the games before the raiding parties arrived.[22]

The way Pendergast had gained police protection for the illegal activities in his saloons is easy to understand. Marcy K. Brown, the influential county politician who persuaded Governor Stone to appoint a new board of police commissioners hostile to Speers, had been defeated in a power struggle the previous summer at the Democratic County Convention. The big fight in the convention had been over the nomination for county prosecuting attorney. Brown and the delegates he controlled voted for Frank G. Johnson. Jim Pendergast, on the other hand, joined forces with the Ninth

Ward politician, Joe Shannon. Together, Pendergast and Shannon had enough delegates to defeat Brown's man, and get their own candidate, J. H. Bremmerman, nominated.

Brown, who had seldom found his power in the county so successfully challenged, realized that he must form an alliance with at least one of the rising young bosses from Kansas City. He decided to try Pendergast, and the two men agreed on a compromise. Pendergast was to support Brown in the next county battle, and Brown was to use his influence to get the police force revamped. Pendergast would help select the new policemen, and Brown promised to use his influence to get the gambling protected in Pendergast's two saloons. Thus, the next spring, less than four weeks after Brown began pressuring Governor Stone to have Chief Speers removed, Jim Pendergast abandoned his alliance with Joe Shannon and supported Brown for re-election to the chairmanship of the Democratic County Committee instead of Shannon's candidate, George Shelley.

Soon, though, Pendergast was unhappy with his new ally because Brown failed to do all that he promised. The rising young ward boss, according to a newspaper reporter, had been promised the right to appoint more of the members to the revamped police force than Brown ultimately allowed.[23] But Pendergast's gambling games were being protected by the police, and any bitterness that existed over patronage was gone by summer. The First Ward alderman and Brown fought side by side in an unsuccessful effort to prevent the election of George Shelley to the chair of the county committee. When Shelley was elected, Pendergast and Brown took their men and stormed out of the meeting. The two bosses refused to recognize the new chairman and they kept the county Democracy split almost until Christmas. The refusal of Brown and Pendergast to support Shannon's candidate paid off. In December, Shelley resigned the chairmanship to which he had been fairly elected. A compromise candidate agreeable to both factions was soon selected.[24]

The alliance with Brown allowed Pendergast to keep the gambling rooms open with only a minimum of police interference. This freedom the big saloonkeeper had not enjoyed before. But the co-operation of the police force brought its problems too. A Kansas City police judge, James Jones, made known his opposition to the gambling in Kansas City. The A.P.A. Republicans nominated Jones for mayor in 1896, and he ran on a platform which pledged to run Ed Findley, the gamekeeper at Pendergast's two saloons, out of Kansas City.

The 1896 election campaign, though based on opposition to gambling, did not discourage Alderman Jim. He ran for re-election anyway. And the vociferous attacks on the police-protected games in his saloons had no apparent effect. The A.P.A.-controlled Republicans again swept the city election, leaving only five lower house posts to the Democrats. Jim Pendergast, however, took one of the five seats for himself, as he trounced his A.P.A. opponent with 632 votes to 372.

It was not at all surprising that "Big Jim" had won again, for even though he was busier than ever before, especially with his first active involvement in county politics, he continued to aid his constituents. The Negroes, for example, who populated a large portion of the First Ward, were undoubtedly impressed when Alderman Jim took the time and effort to put up bail bond for a Negro.[25]

While Pendergast looked out for the special interests of his people in the West Bottoms, he also worked for the general welfare of the city and gained even more prestige. His stand on the gas company franchise illustrated this. In 1895 Kansas Citians were paying $1.60 per 1000 cubic feet of gas to the Philadelphia Gas Company, which held the gas franchise. The company thought it could count on Pendergast's vote when it was time for a franchise renewal. But Pendergast, according to the *Star's* bold headline, "STOOD BY THE CITY AT A CRITICAL MOMENT." With a picture of the big alderman on the front page, the *Star* praised Pendergast for voting against the "trust" and casting the deciding vote in favor of the Dollar Gas Company, which promised to deliver 1000 cubic feet of gas for $1.00.[26] A saving such as this was not only important to hotel-owners like Pendergast; it was important to home-owners all over the city. The reduction was especially important in 1895, because the nation was in the midst of a depression.

During Pendergast's second term in the lower house, he also spoke out for such important issues as lower telephone rates, which were badly needed in Kansas City. On another occasion, he voted for a resolution to appropriate $25,000 to purchase a thirty-three-acre estate for a city park. Although the resolution did not pass the lower house, Pendergast had put himself on record as a supporter of public improvements for Kansas City. [27]

Probably the most significant example of Pendergast's labors during his second term in office concerned the passage of two charter amendments: one for the purchase of a water works plant, and the other for financing the construction of parks and boulevards. Since the 1870's many citizens had been demanding parks and boulevards, as well as a municipally owned water works. These two issues were drawn up in the form of charter amendments and placed before the people for their adoption or rejection in a special election in June 1895. Pendergast gave his full support to the amendments. In fact, he joined a group referred to as "the general committee of friends of the park and water works amendments." After working with the committee in his ward, Alderman Jim told a newspaper reporter that

> nearly every voter in the ward is for the amendments. I think that the amendments will carry by an overwhelming majority. I can find scarcely anyone who is against them. I am in favor of them and have always been so, as my official acts in the city council show.[28]

No one could have known more about what the First Ward would do on election day than the "King of the First." Pendergast had been correct. The amendments were ratified in the First Ward by a six-to-one majority. Hardly anyone had opposed the issues that Jim Pendergast had requested them to support. His ability to bring voters into line in the West Bottoms seemed incredible. The way he had gathered support for the amendments he backed, and the way he had kept the Republican landsides in the past two city elections from touching his ward amazed those who did not understand the source of his popularity. The following description of the Alderman, written by one of his contemporaries, helps one understand why he had the devoted support of his West Bottoms' neighbors:

> He had a big heart, was charitable and liberal. . . . No deserving man, woman or child that appealed to "Jim" Pendergast went away empty handed, and this is saying a great deal, as he was continually giving aid and help to the poor and unfortunate. The extent of his bounty was never known, as he made it an inviolable rule that no publicity should be given to his philanthropy. There never was a winter in the last twenty years that he did not circulate among the poor of the West Bottoms, ascertaining their needs, and after his visit there were no empty larders. Grocers, butchers, bakers and coal men had unlimited orders to see that there was no suffering among the poor of the West Bottoms, and to send the bills to "Jim" Pendergast.[29]

The personal favors that Pendergast performed for his constituents, his actions within the council chamber which benefited many of them, and the police department patronage which aided at least a few, all helped Alderman Jim dominate the First Ward politically. But the big Irishman was not satisfied with being just the leader of the West Bottoms. He wanted to extend his power into the North End.

2

The Boss of the West Bottoms
and North End

Throughout the years that Pendergast was perfecting his organization in the West Bottoms, he was laying the groundwork for political control of the North End. The first inroad into North End politics came in 1891 when the Alderman purchased a saloon in that area. While still retaining a saloon and a hotel in the West Bottoms, Pendergast was now in business in the Second Ward, where he could make new contacts and friends. Only one block from the court house and city hall, his new saloon soon became the headquarters for city officeholders, as well as lawyers and gamblers.[1]

The North End power elite was made up of the men who ran the liquor and gambling interests there. Pendergast quickly surrounded himself with these men, and through his business he early became associated with the liquor interests. Many of his friends came from this same circle—Martin Regan, for example, the North End alderman and saloonkeeper, vacationed with Alderman Jim. And John Moran, another saloonkeeper and North End politician, became one of Jim's close friends. It was Moran whom Pendergast defended in the lower house when some members urged his removal from office because of his arrest for election fraud.

Jim Pendergast's ties with the gambling interests were even stronger than with the liquor interests. As we have seen, the gambler Ed Findley operated large dice games from both of Jim's saloons. Although Findley made his headquarters at Jim's North End saloon, his gambling combine spread all over the North End. Billy Christie's saloon, for example, was only one of several other locations for Findley's games. It was Pendergast's alliance with Marcy K. Brown which brought police protection to organized gambling in 1895. The police department also aided the gambling combine. A free-lance gambling house operator in the North End testified that Ed Findley had warned him to join the combine or be raided by the police. The gambler refused to join Findley and soon was raided.[2]

The gambling interests operated on a large scale in Kansas City. Pendergast's North End saloon had several tables and twenty-two men operating the games. And his saloon in the West Bottoms had four dice tables and a large staff also. Disturbed over the increase in gambling, the Kansas City Civic Federation had been gathering information about the gambling machine, which had greatly expanded after Chief of Police Speers was ousted from office in 1895. Just how reliable the information gathered by this reform group was, it is impossible to say. The group reported that almost $800,-000 was grossed annually by the combine. A spokesman for the Civic Federation said that their figures tallied with information gathered by "entirely different sources."[3]

In any case, the extent of the gambling was so vast a few months after Speers's dismissal, that it produced a severe reaction from many quarters in Kansas City. Ironically, it was the reaction against the gambling interests that enabled Jim Pendergast to become the political boss of the North End.

It all began in August 1896 at the Democratic County Convention. Jim Pendergast was still allied with Marcy K. Brown. Joe Shannon, who had no interests whatever in the gambling combine, did not hesitate to endorse reformer Frank Lowe from the Tenth Ward. Lowe, a young Kansas City lawyer, had the delegates of the large Tenth Ward at his disposal. To get himself nominated for prosecuting attorney, Lowe was willing to support Shannon's ticket if Shannon would in turn support him. The trade was made and Shannon and Lowe found enough other support to nominate the entire ticket.[4]

Pendergast had supported James A. Reed, another young Kansas City attorney, for prosecuting attorney. Pendergast had been able to deliver the First Ward delegates, but Brown, who tried to deliver some other delegates for Reed, lost many old supporters to Shannon. It was a devastating blow to Brown, who had been a powerful county boss. The Kansas City newspapers all celebrated his fall from power, and heralded the rise of Joe Shannon.

As prosecuting attorney, Lowe rigorously pursued his campaign promises. The mayor of Kansas City, James Jones, had been fighting a battle against the police-protected gambling at Pendergast's saloons and other places since his election a few months earlier. Lowe promised his support in helping to clean up the city by running the gamblers out of town. During his first month as prosecuting attorney, the young reformer obtained fifty-seven indictments from the grand jury against gamblers whom the police had been shielding. One of the fifty-seven was Ed Findley, who was charged with operating games in both of Pendergast's saloons. When he appeared in court, the judge set the bond at $2000, which was put up by Pendergast.[5]

Lowe's energetic prosecution of the gamblers stimulated intense opposition in the saloon- and gambling-controlled North End. With Brown stripped of his power after the last county campaign, Pendergast organized and strengthened what remained of Brown's machine in the North End. He was able to do so because, being a part of the saloon and gambling interests in the North End himself, he was trusted. But Pendergast had yet another advantage in rebuilding the organization. The North End leaders knew that they must defeat Shannon in the next convention in order to get rid of reformer Lowe. Consequently, they were willing to follow Pendergast because it was obvious that his West Bottoms delegation, plus their own, might be able to defeat Shannon at the next county convention.

William R. Nelson's *Kansas City Star* seldom missed anything significant that was going on in Kansas City. This occasion was no exception. Nearly a month before the Democratic primaries and county convention, the *Star* had discovered the rise of "A NEW DEMOCRATIC BOSS." [6] Pendergast had managed to reorganize under his own leadership nearly all of Brown's followers. Likewise, he brought into the combine John P. O'Neil, who was quite important because he had a large following in the Fifth and Tenth wards. O'Neil was also valuable because he could help in the North End; like Pendergast, he had a business located there.

The *Star* was correct. Pendergast had come to the front as a leader, which he aptly demonstrated in the Democratic County Convention in the summer of 1898. Pendergast met the Shannon faction under a big circus tent in Independence, Missouri. The Pendergast crowd, shrewdly trading votes with county leaders, proceeded to unseat Frank Lowe and nominate James A. Reed for prosecuting attorney. According to one newspaper account, Lowe's defeat was due mainly "to the fact that he made vigorous prosecutions against the gamblers' combine." [7] Joe Shannon was asked the reason for his setback, and he explained that "the defeat of Lowe is a hard blow but is easily explained. With the police machine, the brewers and the gamblers against him there was no chance for him." [8]

These assertions were largely correct. Pendergast had the support of the delegates from his own First Ward, but he also had been backed by the delegates in the Second and Sixth wards, which made up the North End. Pendergast's heelers at the convention, who brought the delegates in line, were representatives of the gambling and saloon interests, such as Pinky Blitz, Ed Findley, and "Fighting Jim" Pryor. Pinky Blitz was a notorious gambler and politician who had just served a two-year term in the state prison.

"Fighting Jim" Pryor was a riotous saloonkeeper for whom Pendergast provided bail on several occasions. And Ed Findley, of course, was the dean of the North End gamblers.[9]

Thus, by 1898, Alderman Jim Pendergast had established himself as the new leader of the North End. He was still the undisputed boss of the First Ward, as he had demonstrated by his third re-election to the lower house. But now he had another neighborhood to maintain; and once he had arrived he had no intention of letting any of his following slip away. One way that he ingratiated himself with the people in both neighborhoods was aptly described a few years later in the *Kansas City Times:*

> Alderman Jim's political power was established by his generosity, his big heartedness, his readiness to do favors for the "boys," to "go to the front" for one who was in trouble, get jobs and do various little acts of kindness for those who were in need.[10]

Pendergast himself agreed, in retrospect, with this interpretation:

> I've been called a boss. All there is to it is having friends, doing things for people, and then later on they'll do things for you. . . . You can't coerce people into doing things for you—you can't make them vote for you. I never coerced anybody in my life. Wherever you see a man bulldozing anybody he don't last long.[11]

An important vehicle which was used by Pendergast for making friends and doing favors was the police department. It brought him friends by affording protection to the North End gambling interests and making jobs available to his followers. Reformers in Kansas City were not oblivious to this source of Pendergast's strength; indeed, they tried to destroy it.

Soon after Pendergast had extended his power into the North End, such outspoken opponents of his as Mayor Jones started a campaign for home rule of the police department. It was clear that if the past was any guide for the future, as long as a Democrat was governor of Missouri, the most powerful Democrats in Kansas City would be given the control of the police department. Thus Mayor Jones was sure that the only way to take the department from Jim Pendergast's hands was to enact municipal home rule. The Missouri Constitution of 1875 had granted all cities with a population of 100,000 or over the right to draw up their own charters, which could be enacted by a three-fifths majority vote.[12] Kansas City received a home rule charter in 1889. Now, all that was needed to establish municipal control over the police was a three-fifths majority vote to amend the charter.

Mayor Jones was not alone in wanting to destroy Pendergast's political power. Nelson Crews, a Republican and a well-known leader of Kansas City's Negro community, also wanted to bring the police department under home rule. Likewise, William Rockhill Nelson, the editor of the *Star,* backed the home rule movement through his newspaper. These men were only some of the diverse elements which supported the movement and succeeded in placing a proposed amendment to the charter before the voters in September 1898.

If anyone had doubted the strength of "Boss" Pendergast before this special election, they did not afterwards. When the election returns came in, all but four of the city's fourteen wards voted in favor of home rule. The four wards that voted against the proposal were Pendergast's First Ward in the West Bottoms, wards Two and Six which made up the North End; plus the independent Thirteenth Ward on the southeast edge of the city limits. The Thirteenth made little difference though, because it cast only a few votes altogether. And out of the few cast, only fourteen more votes were against the amendment than for it. In marked contrast, Pendergast's three wards delivered three-to-one majorities against the amendment, and the city-wide three-fifths majority necessary for passage was not attained. By turning the voters in the river wards against the amendment, Pendergast had crushed a movement which challenged his control over an important segment of his political machine.

The boss's show of strength in this special election was only the first of a series of impressive demonstrations. The year 1900 was one of the most significant that Pendergast ever experienced in perfecting his growing political organization. In February, preparations for the ensuing city election were being made by the leaders of the local Democracy. As had happened before, and would happen again in the future, Jim Pendergast and Joe Shannon began to struggle for power. Pendergast wanted to nominate the mayoralty candidate by ballot primary, but Shannon wanted the nomination made in the city convention.[13] It was clear that Pendergast would have the advantage in nominating his candidate for mayor in a primary, because he could count on so many votes in the river wards. Shannon, on the other hand, had demonstrated that at times he could not even deliver the votes in his own Ninth Ward. Therefore Shannon knew that he would have a better chance of naming the candidate in a convention, where delegates could be traded and deals could be made.

When the problem of nominating the mayoralty candidate came before the meeting of the Democratic City Central Committee, to which Pendergast and Shannon both belonged, Alderman Jim's desires were followed. With the help of Bernard Corrigan, the wealthy president of the Metropolitan Street Railway Company, Pendergast was able to produce a majority vote for a ballot primary.[14] This early victory was indicative of what was to follow.

For the Democratic primary election, Alderman Jim selected thirty-eight-year-old James A. Reed to carry the Pendergast banner. Pendergast's successful candidate for prosecuting attorney in 1898, Reed was known throughout the city as an eloquent stump speaker. Joe Shannon called upon George M. Shelley, twice elected mayor of Kansas City, to lead his faction's ticket. A third candidate, A. L. O. Schueler, entered the campaign with the pledge that he would be the tool of no boss. When the votes were in it was clear that Pendergast was much more powerful than Shannon. Reed, who would one day make a name for himself as a Senator, carried every ward in the city except Shannon's Ninth Ward, and he lost it by only sixty-one votes out of almost 1000 cast. Reed's biggest majorities were in Pendergast's river wards, where he carried the First Ward twenty-five-to-one (440 to 18) and the Second Ward ten-to-one (440 to 44). In the Sixth Ward Reed won 348 out of the 438 votes cast. The rest of the city's wards, on the other hand, did not give the young lawyer such large pluralities.

In the Democratic City Convention which followed the primary, the remainder of the ticket was selected. Pendergast combined again with Bernard Corrigan as well as with Joe Heim, who was one of the owners of the large Heim Brewery in Kansas City. These three men selected most of the ticket, but it was clear that Pendergast had the upper hand. When a dispute over one upper house candidate arose, Pendergast's preference was ultimately accepted. Alderman Jim allowed Heim and Corrigan to pick some upper house candidates in return for their support on the remainder of the ticket.

Once the ticket was nominated, "Big Jim" put his machine into action, hoping to defeat the local Republicans who had dominated the mayoralty and a majority of the city council seats for the past six years. Pendergast left nothing to chance in preparation for the campaign. It was the first one in which a major attempt to organize the Italians was publicized. Pendergast had Joe Damico, the "King of Little Italy," give campaign speeches in Italian to the North End Italians. Mike Heim, a brother of Pendergast's ally Joe Heim, was busy serving free beer to the German voters all over the city. The gambling element of the city's Negro population had been told that a vote for Reed meant less police interference with their illegal activities.[15] And ever since Bernard Corrigan entered the picture, Pendergast's campaign fund, according to a local newspaper, "had plenty of money and money is nowhere more useful than in politics." [16]

From his North End saloon, Jim Pendergast directed every motion of his expanding political organization. Just before the election of 1900, the *Kansas City Star* described "PENDERGAST AT HIS POST" in an editorial:

In these stirring times there is much activity at the Pendergast headquarters on lower Main Street. The free lunch table shows unusual affluence and awakens special appreciation. The struggle for supremacy between the odor which arises from the onions and the garlic bolognas and the aroma which continually ascends from the bar is more than ordinarily acute.

In this pungent and vitalizing atmosphere, Pendergast stands and promulgates his wise counsel. What need, indeed, has he for halls or stages or rostrums? Here gather the candidates, to learn how the battle is waging. Here assemble the leaders to confer together. Here come the humble toilers in the Democratic vineyard to receive their instructions. . . . Pendergast is not seen going about much in the present campaign. That would be a needless waste of time. He would miss more Democrats by going away than he would see. It is not necessary for him to move out of his place to find anybody he can use or wants to help. They all go to him. The post of duty is the place for Pendergast. If his ward wants him it has but to call at the back or the front door and he is ready.[17]

Pendergast's direction of the 1900 campaign reached a climax on the eve of the election. Kansas City's Convention Hall was filled almost to capacity with 10,000 men and women present for the final Democratic rally. The First Ward crowd, which had unanimously nominated "Big Jim" for the fifth time, came into the hall carrying two large banners. One banner was inscribed "We stand by honest Jim Pendergast," and the other one read "We are for the two Jims," meaning of course Jim Pendergast and Jim Reed.[18] The local Republican newspaper, the *Journal*, looked upon the meeting with disdain. It was the largest Democratic meeting of the campaign, asserted the *Journal*, but only because "scores of Italians were herded by 'King Joe' Damico and the riff-raff of the North end swarmed into the hall." [19] But to Alderman Jim, as William Reddig reminds us,

> the inhabitants of the slums, the floaters in the flophouses, the shanty dwellers of the East Bottoms, the laboring men in the West Bottoms and the people of Little Italy were not the teeming masses so luridly described in the literature of the period as

the flotsam and jetsam of society. They were personal friends of
Alderman Jim Pendergast. He liked to listen to their stories and
took a genuine interest in their problems. He got them jobs on
the city or county payrolls or with business friends of the organization.[20]

These friends of Jim Pendergast's, whom he had been taking
care of personally and through his organization, demonstrated
their appreciation on election day. The West Bottoms' dwellers
returned Alderman Jim to the lower house with the largest plural-
ity he had ever received. And James A. Reed beat William Brown,
his Republican opponent for mayor, in all but five of the city's
fourteen wards. It was clear, though, that the future Senator owed
his victory to Pendergast. As the *Star* pointed out, "Reed's heaviest
majorities came from the portion of the city that is in the West
Bottoms and north of Eighth Street. Farther south the heads of the
tickets divided the vote practically equally between them." [21]

Reed's victory immeasurably aided the Pendergast machine, for
this was the first time that Pendergast had had the pleasure of
working with a Democratic mayor since he had become a power
in Kansas City politics. Reed was Pendergast's man, and within a
very short time, he began furnishing Pendergast with patronage for
his machine. More patronage was now available to the politician
than ever before. Alderman Jim wanted and received the appointment of his younger brother, Tom, to the position of superintendent
of streets. This was a coveted position because the superintendent
at that time handled more patronage than any city official other
than the mayor. The superintendent employed over two hundred
men and thirty teams of horses for street work. But the street department was not all that Reed's victory had made available; the
fire department fell to the spoils system too. Within a month after
Reed took office, Republican firemen were being removed to make
room for loyal Democrats.[22]

There were many city hall jobs which went to the Pendergast
machine, such as the position of deputy license inspector for
Kansas City. That job went to one of Pendergast's ward heelers in

the Second Ward, Charles Clark. When all of this new patronage was placed at Pendergast's disposal, he was unquestionably the most powerful boss in the city. Not only did the organization control street department and fire department jobs by 1900, as well as many other city jobs; it also dominated the police force. Between 1900 and 1902, Jim Pendergast named 123 out of the 173 patrolmen on the force.[23]

Thus by 1900 Pendergast was the manager of a political machine which was more encompassing than anything Kansas City had seen before. It appeared that he was well on his way to becoming the boss of Kansas City, with a powerful machine reaching into every corner of that growing metropolis. But Alderman Jim was to sustain some serious setbacks which left him at his retirement in 1910 what he had been just prior to the election of 1900: the boss of the West Bottoms and North End.

The first reversal came in the fall of 1900 when Pendergast attempted to name the county ticket again, as he had in 1898. However, in the two years between conventions some important changes had come about. While Pendergast could count on a generous percentage of the city vote, he could no longer compete with Joe Shannon in the county. During the two years between the Democratic county conventions, Pendergast had been concentrating on the city campaigns. Shannon, on the other hand, had been seeking supporters on the county level. Several of Shannon's relatives held important county offices, and his followers had obtained thirty or forty positions in the county court house.[24]

Consequently, Joe Shannon, with his increasing influence, had packed the Democratic County Committee with a majority of his own men, and managed to elect the chairman, Frank P. Sebree. The result of Shannon's victory was that in the county convention the committee seated Shannon's delegates from all of the wards which had contested delegations. Pendergast lost his temper when his delegates were ignored and Shannon's were seated. The big Irishman called his delegates together and they withdrew from the convention to nominate their own ticket.

Many efforts were made by independent Democrats to work out a compromise between the Shannon and Pendergast factions, but all to no avail. Therefore the Democratic State Central Committee went to Kansas City in an effort to reunite the Jackson County Democracy. The committee listened to both sides of the story and finally decided that a new primary election should be called, and a new convention held too. Shannon refused to follow the suggestions to participate in the primary. He asserted that his ticket was the legally elected one and carried the dispute to the Missouri Supreme Court. The court ruled in Shannon's favor and awarded him the right to put his ticket in the field. According to the court, the State Central Committee possessed only advisory powers and was thus "without jurisdiction in the matter." [25] When the Supreme Court's decision was announced, Pendergast said he would abide by the decision but that his faction would "keep their coats on and allow the other crowd to do the work." [26]

Pendergast's refusal to work for the Shannon nominees proved disastrous for the Democratic ticket. Instead of the river wards turning out their usual large majorities, they were of little help. Pendergast's First Ward, which since 1892 had produced large majorities, gave the Democratic ticket about a three-to-two majority. And the Second Ward split its votes evenly between the two parties. Because the river wards did not deliver the usual majorities, the entire Jackson County Republican ticket was elected. Thus, while Pendergast had been stopped by Shannon in his attempt to dominate the county convention again, Shannon could not get the ticket elected. Both bosses, therefore, were forced to compromise.

The Shannon-Pendergast split and the consequent Republican victory in Jackson County led to the birth of the famous and long-lived Fifty-Fifty compromise. This compromise between the factions, while not observed in every city and county election, was accepted by both factions in many elections throughout the days of Jim Pendergast's reign and continued on into the era of Tom Pendergast. Fifty-Fifty was actually a setback for Alderman Jim.

In 1898 he had been able to name almost the entire Democratic ticket, and he had left Shannon with hardly anything. By 1900, however, because of Shannon's growth in county-wide strength, Pendergast was forced to accept the Fifty-Fifty compromise.

This was only the first reversal that Jim Pendergast experienced after 1900. The defeat of the county ticket had cost him some valuable patronage, which he could have used to bolster his already strong position in the West Bottoms and North End, as well as expand his power into other areas of the city or county. Added to this disappointment was the loss of his control over the police department. While William J. Stone from 1893 to 1897, and Lon V. Stephens from 1897 to 1901, were governors of Missouri, first Brown and then Pendergast dictated the selection of many members of the Board of Police Commissioners. By 1900 Pendergast virtually controlled the police force. But when Alexander M. Dockery became governor in 1901 the situation took a marked turn. When Dockery entered the State House, Robert L. Gregory, James A. Reed, and Hugh C. Ward were the members of the Board of Police Commissioners. All three of these men were members of the Pendergast faction and close friends of Jim Pendergast's. As long as they were on the board, whatever Pendergast asked was done. In 1902 their two-year terms ended, and it was time for the governor to appoint two new members, the mayor always being the third person on the board. So while Pendergast's man, Mayor Reed, would remain a member if he could be re-elected in 1902, Pendergast still needed to get at least one other friend of his on the board to have a majority.

In January 1902 Pendergast began pressuring Governor Dockery to reappoint R. L. Gregory to the police board. Jim Reed even went personally to the state capitol in Jefferson City to put in a word for Gregory. Governor Dockery came to Kansas City in late January to discuss the selection of the new appointees with the leaders of the local Democracy. As soon as he arrived in Kansas City the governor was visited in his room at the Baltimore Hotel by Pendergast. According to the *Kansas City Star* "The big boss of the

North end ventured out in the snow to lay down his one proposition. . . . He asks for Gregory . . . he has no second choice." [27]
Dockery faced quite a dilemma, for Shannon was as much opposed to Gregory's appointment as Pendergast was for it.

On February 10, the governor had made his choice. He appointed Frank Sebree and William T. Kemper to replace Hugh Ward and R. L. Gregory. This was a blow to "Big Jim" because Sebree was a Shannon man, and Kemper was far from being a Pendergast follower. Pendergast had worked with Kemper out of necessity at times, but basically they were political enemies. It was Kemper, after all, who in 1899 had founded the Jackson County Democratic Club, which was a faction independent of both Shannon and Pendergast.

In 1902, then, Pendergast lost his influence over two of the three members of the Board of Police Commissioners. When the term of that board was drawing to a close, Alderman Jim again solicited the aid of Governor Dockery by asking him to appoint R. L. Gregory to the new board. Again Dockery refused to be pressured by Pendergast, and he appointed D. J. Dean, who was not associated with either the Pendergast or the Shannon faction. Furthermore, in April 1904 a Republican was elected mayor of Kansas City. Thus when the new mayor, Jay H. Neff, joined the police board, Pendergast's influence with the police department was nothing but a memory. In August 1904 the *Kansas City Star* asserted that "for many years 'Pendergast faction' and 'police faction' have been synonymous in Kansas City . . . but he [Pendergast] has been crowded to the second table in police matters." [28]

The control of the police department taken from him, Pendergast lost most of the city-wide strength which he had gained by 1900, as well as much of his bargaining power. As early as July 1902 the Kansas City *Journal* recognized Pendergast's diminishing power:

> When Ward and Gregory were police commissioners, the mere appearance of the big alderman from the first ward at police headquarters set every member of the "fo'ce," from Chief Hayes

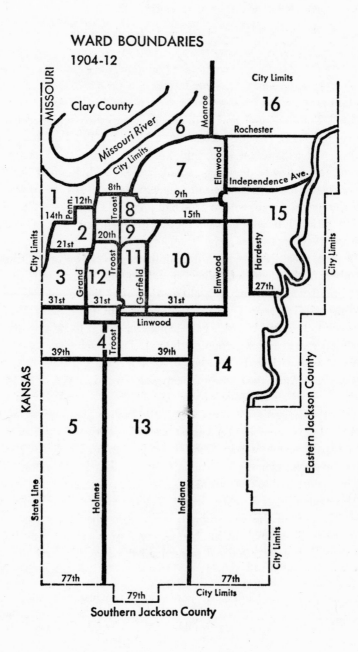

WARD BOUNDARIES
1904-12

MISSOURI

Clay County

Missouri River

City Limits

City Limits

16

Monroe

6

Rochester

7

Elmwood

Independence Ave.

1

Penn. 12th

8th

9th

8

15

14th

Troost

15th

21st

2

20th

9

Hardesty

Grand

Troost

11

10

3

12

Garfield

Elmwood

31st

31st

31st

27th

Linwood

4

Troost

39th

39th

14

KANSAS

5

13

State Line

Holmes

Indiana

Eastern Jackson County

77th

79th

77th

City Limits

City Limits

Southern Jackson County

to the driver of the patrol wagon, to knocking his head on the floor. Great was the police machine and "Big Jim" was its prophet.

But since the appointment of Sebree and Kemper as police commissioners, Pendergast's power has been rapidly declining. Two years ago he absolutely controlled the Democratic city convention and nominated his candidate, Reed, for mayor. Last spring, the police having passed out of his control, he had to divide the spoils of the convention with his old enemy, Shannon. In the recent county convention he was so powerless that he could not even get his friend and candidate for governor, Reed, elected delegate to the state convention. And now the commissioners . . . are swiftly cutting off the heads of his friends on the police department.[29]

By 1904 the chance of Pendergast's returning to the powerful position which he had held from 1900 to 1902 was gone. Governor Dockery was followed in office by Joseph W. Folk and Herbert S. Hadley, reformers out to destroy the kind of politics upon which Jim Pendergast had thrived. Likewise, after Jim Reed vacated the mayor's office in 1904, the Republicans moved in and stayed until 1908. Thus Pendergast had lost not only his patronage from the police department but also the valuable patronage that was at the disposal of the mayor. But Pendergast was not destroyed completely. The Republican *Journal's* prediction of the "DECLINE AND FALL OF PENDERGAST"[30] was far from correct. Although the big boss had fallen far from the pinnacle he had reached by 1902, he maintained his hold over the West Bottoms and the North End.

Alderman Jim's firm grip on the West Bottoms and the North End was demonstrated on several occasions before bad health curtailed his political activity. In 1904, he was elected to represent the First Ward in the lower house for the seventh time. This election illustrated Pendergast's strength in the North End as well as the West Bottoms because the ward boundaries had been changed just prior to the election. The First Ward of 1904 included all of the West Bottoms as it had before, but it annexed the

entire Second Ward from the North End, as well as two precincts
of the much more heavily Republican Third Ward. The Sixth Ward
remained intact, embracing the eastern half of the North End,
which the Second Ward had never encompassed.

Pendergast was opposed by another Democrat in this 1904
election, and that was the first and last time that such a futile attempt to oust "Big Jim" was made. Alderman Jim received 1513
votes; his Democratic opponent, Daniel Rice, 383. The Republican
candidate, Edward Zola, won only 288 votes. Although the city
elected a Republican, J. H. Neff, as mayor by a more than 2000-
vote majority, Pendergast faithfully delivered large neighborhood
majorities for the Democratic candidate, William T. Kemper. In
the First Ward, Kemper received 1487 votes to Neff's 420, and in
the Sixth, Kemper was given 1341 and Neff an even 600.

A year later Pendergast again demonstrated his strength when
the river wards' votes helped defeat the proposed Charter of 1905.
James Peters, a lawyer who was secretary to the Board of Free-
holders which drafted the proposal, pointed out that there was a
demand for a new charter. The demand had developed because
the Charter of 1889 had become outmoded. The existing charter,
Peters commented, did not provide the city with many of the
powers it urgently needed. Among the powers that the new charter
would have extended to the city was the right to construct tunnels,
subways, and viaducts between the two Kansas Cities. Likewise,
the city would be granted the power to condemn property for
hospitals, and to levy assessments against railroad property. The
city would also gain the authority to negotiate long-term contracts for such things as garbage collection and street repairs.[31]

The charter proposal provided the city with the above-mentioned
powers, as well as the right to regulate saloon licenses. The city
excise commission would be required to withdraw the saloon
license of any saloonkeeper if at least two property owners on the
same block signed a petition requesting such action. Also, the
proposed charter granted the city the authority to license and tax
all trades, professions, and employments—thus allowing the city

to tax common wage laborers on their earnings. Another article in the 1905 charter called for the creation of a civil service commission, which would control all city employees, and therefore do away with the spoils system.

Alderman Jim was emphatically opposed to the charter proposal. He told a reporter for the Kansas City *World*

> . . . it makes the mayor too powerful. It gives him more power than George Washington had, or the president has, or the governor. . . . If I was mayor and that new charter went into effect I could fix it so that my party would stay in power for fifty years. . . . There's the excise article that says that two men in the block can close up a saloon. I believe the rule of letting the majority decide is a good one. . . . I wouldn't let any commissioners dictate to me. I'd lock my place up first. . . .
>
> And the occupation tax. If someone was to tell all the clerks and men of any other occupation that the council could put a tax of from $10 to $50 a year on them just because they have a job, do you think they would go out and work for the charter? People tell me that that's just put in the charter—not because the council is ever going to pass an ordinance like that. But how are they to guarantee what the council is to do? If they don't want the council to pass a law like that, why don't they keep that section out of the charter? . . . Men ought to go into every ward in Kansas City and show this thing up. It ought to be beat and I'll fight to do it.[32]

Pendergast undoubtedly was opposed to the civil service section of the charter, as well as the saloon closing and occupation tax articles. A local newspaper, which was supporting the charter proposal, stated that Pendergast said to the voter: "You help me and I'll help you. You vote as I tell you to, and when my men are in I will see that you get a job." [33] The *World* asserted that this was a strong argument,

> . . . and it has made Mr. Pendergast a power in local politics. It is not extraordinary that he "views with alarm" a measure that proposes to put a quietus on the practice of doling out the posi-

tions in the public service as rewards for political services rendered to party bosses.[34]

Pendergast could not stand by apathetically and see the spoils system destroyed, nor could he stand by and see his saloon business threatened. "Big Jim" also had to think about the other saloon interests in the river wards which he was representing; and he could not forget the already poorly paid laborers in his wards who were threatened with an occupation tax that very well might ruin them.

Jim Pendergast promised to fight the charter, and that is exactly what he did. Joe Shannon, who looked at the civil service section of the charter in much the same light as Alderman Jim, also put forth all his efforts to defeat the measure. When the votes were counted, the *Journal* reported that the charter had been defeated and the "BOSSES SHANNON AND PENDERGAST [the] ONES WHO DID IT." The paper went on to say that "In Wards Controlled by Them the Good Work Done by Citizens in Other Localities Was Negatived." [35] Most of the residential wards in Kansas City had given a majority of their votes to the charter. Shannon's Ninth Ward on the other hand, voted nearly two-to-one against the proposal. In Pendergast's wards, the majorities against the charter were even greater. In the First Ward the final count was five-to-one against the charter, and in the Sixth the margin was almost four-to-one in opposition to the measure.

The spell that Pendergast had cast over the voters in the West Bottoms and North End was illustrated again several months later when he ran for alderman from the First for the eighth consecutive time. Alderman Jim, who was returned to the lower house, polled 1346 votes to his Republican opponent's 474. Pendergast's strength had become so great in the First Ward that, as A. Theodore Brown phrased it, when he "decided to run in a campaign, it amounted to a decision to continue in office." [36]

Even though Jim Pendergast had lost much of the city hall patronage which he had won by 1900-1902, even though he had been forced to split his county patronage fifty-fifty with Joe Shannon after 1900, it is not difficult to see how he continued to maintain his control over the river wards during the ensuing years. Jim's river ward followers did not forsake him because he no longer had as many jobs to pass out, they loved him just the same. They never forgot the many ways in which the saloonkeeper had helped them.

The devastating flood of 1903 nearly destroyed the river wards. Many families lost their homes and all their possessions. When in despair they looked for aid, and there was Alderman Jim leading the relief work while his own property was being destroyed. Pendergast provided homes and furnishings for many families, and put many of the stricken back on their feet again. He asked the newspaper reporters not to mention his relief work, saying, "It was my own money I spent, and the public is not interested in how I spend my money." [37]

Jim Pendergast's benevolence was not reserved for emergencies like the 1903 flood. Indeed, his kindness was spread among his followers perpetually. The author of *Tom's Town* discovered

> . . . the North Siders went to Pendergast for more than jobs. They went to him when they were in trouble and needed someone to soften the stern hand of justice. Many of them got fuel and other supplies from his precinct captains when they were down and out. Others ate his turkey and trimmings at the free Christmas dinners which he gave for the Old Town derelicts, beginning with fifty guests and growing into the hundreds as the number of drifters increased year after year.[38]

To the river ward unfortunates Pendergast was a savior whose name was revered. When Pendergast called for votes in a local election he could count on the loyal support of his constituency in the West Bottoms and North End. After his election to the lower house in 1906, however, he played a much less active role in Kansas City politics. The alderman's health was beginning to weaken, and he called upon his brother Tom to perform more and more of his strenuous political duties. Thus, even before Alderman Jim retired, Tom Pendergast was well versed in operating the machine he would one day inherit.

3

Tom Pendergast Is Groomed for Leadership

For many years Jim Pendergast's health had not been good. As early as 1900, he was forced to leave his ward and go to El Paso, Texas, where he could rest and rebuild his strength. The following year, Pendergast again left Kansas City in search of health. This time he went to the Minnesota woods for a month's recuperation from the strain of being a businessman and the boss of the river wards. The next winter it was reported that Pendergast was again ill. "Pendergast has a cold," announced the *Star*, "that threatens to develop into pneumonia. . . . His lungs are not strong and he is not fitted to stand a severe attack of cold or pneumonia." [1]

Jim Pendergast's health continued to weaken throughout the years that he sat in the lower house of Kansas City's common council. After his re-election in 1906 he continued his duties in the council, but began delegating the chores of managing the machine to his younger brother Tom.

Sixteen years younger than Alderman Jim, Tom had come with two of his brothers, Mike and John, to Kansas City from St. Joseph, Missouri, in 1890. The three young men were to become important parts of the Pendergast machine, proving to be especially useful in organizing ward clubs. It was Tom Pendergast though, who early proved to be the most talented of the three younger brothers. He was twenty years old when he arrived in Kansas City, and was put to work as a bookkeeper in the Pendergast saloons.[2] The young bookkeeper looked much like his older brother, having a stocky frame, round face, thick neck, and massive mustache. Tom Pendergast, however, could be easily distinguished from Jim. Tom had lighter hair, and more of it, and, in contrast to the mild baritone of the First Ward Alderman, his voice was deep and demanding.

A member of the Shannon faction recalled that in the early days, "we looked on cunning, resourceful Jim as smartest of the smart, and dismissed Tom . . . as a thick-skulled, heavy-jowled oaf."[3] Tom Pendergast was undoubtedly no sagacious politician when he first made his appearance in Kansas City's river wards, but the young man soon developed into one. Under the tutelage of Kansas City's most powerful boss, brother Tom learned to direct the Pendergast machine. For sixteen years Jim instructed him in the ABC's of machine politics in Kansas City. As an election worker in the river ward precincts, Tom Pendergast learned how to use his fists and earn the respect of the West Bottoms and North End laboring-men. Similarly, in the Pendergast saloons, Tom learned still more about the mechanics of the Pendergast organization, and how it was administered. There he met and talked with the members of the Pendergast political hierarchy.[4]

In a short time, the young student of machine politics graduated from his bookkeeping post in his brother's saloons to his first political office; he was appointed deputy county marshal of Jackson County in 1896. In 1900, when Alderman Jim reached the acme of his political strength, Mayor James A. Reed appointed Tom to the patronage-laden office of superintendent of streets.

Tom Pendergast remained the superintendent of streets in Kansas City for only two years, for in the Democratic County Convention of 1902, he was nominated for county marshal. The ease of his nomination in the county convention was a direct re-

sult of the Fifty-Fifty compromise between the Shannon and Pendergast factions. Shannon selected most of the names on the county
ticket, but Tom Pendergast was nominated for county marshal,
and Jim Pendergast was selected as a delegate to the state convention.

The Democratic candidate was no stranger to Jackson County
politics in 1902, because his brother had shown him around the
county as well as the city. As early as 1896 for example, Tom Pendergast was serving on the executive committe of the Democratic
County Committee, and he had been deputy county marshal for
two years as well. Thus Tom Pendergast was well known in county
politics by 1902. His own familiarity with county politics, plus the
backing of Joe Shannon and Jim Pendergast, gave him quite an
advantage.

The Goats, as the Pendergast followers were called, and the
Rabbits, as the Shannon men were called, rallied behind Tom Pendergast in 1902 and he was elected by a 5240 vote majority.[5] Again
in 1904 and 1906, Tom was nominated for county marshal in the
Democratic county conventions, which were harmoniously conducted on the Fifty-Fifty basis. But in neither November election
was he able to survive the Republican landslides which buried the
Democratic county tickets. On each occasion, the river wards delivered large majorities for him, but most of the other wards in the
city, as well as the county districts, went to the Republican candidates.

Even though Tom Pendergast was defeated in 1904 and 1906,
his two-year term as county marshal had been significant for both
himself and Jim Pendergast. As county marshal between 1902 and
1904, he had gained respect and popularity from certain groups. A
Republican Negro newspaper in Kansas City put aside its par-
tisanship in 1906 to speak out for the younger Pendergast:

> Mr. Pendergast's term as marshal established a new era in
> penal progress. He stood for the Negro as well as the white man.
> No cruel treatment of prisoners. No jail scandals. . . . Let us
> try him again.[6]

As another example, at Christmas time in 1903, Tom used his own money to purchase fourteen turkeys and all the trimmings to brighten the holiday for the 120 inmates in the Jackson County jail. This sort of conduct had a dual effect. It added not only to the immediate stature of the Pendergast machine in places like the rough and tumble river wards; but also to the number of men who would not forget Tom when he ultimately took over the Goat faction.

By 1906, Tom Pendergast was well versed in the politics of Kansas City and Jackson County. He therefore was qualified to take on some of the responsibility which was being delegated to him increasingly by his ailing brother. As we have seen, although Alderman Jim continued to occupy his seat in the lower house until April 1910, his political activities outside of the city council decreased after 1906.

Jim Pendergast attended the Democratic County Convention in August 1906, but this was one of the last important political meetings, outside of the city council, that he was to attend. In the 1906 convention, he and Joe Shannon agreed to another Fifty-Fifty compromise, just as they had been doing with some semblance of regularity since 1901.

The year 1907, without any city or county elections, was rather quiet for the local Democracy. The one big event of the year, however, the meeting of the Democratic County Committee, was held without Alderman Jim's presence. His absence was so unusual that it amazed the *Kansas City Star*.[7] But the saloonkeeper's health had grown much worse, and he was in Los Angeles attempting to regain his strength.

Two months later, when the politicians began discussing candidates for the spring campaign of 1908, the Kansas City *World* declared: "It is doubtful whether Pendergast will care to run for alderman of the 1st ward again. He has served the ward in the council for years. His health has been bad."[8] Pendergast himself said: "The doctor told me not to get into politics, and anything the doc'ie says goes with Jim."[9] But Jim Pendergast did not follow the doctor's advice. He let his followers talk him into running for the lower house from the First Ward once more. This time he did stay away from the sweat and toil of the campaign much more than he had in the past. Instead of soliciting votes himself, he had his brother do most of the work. The alderman told a newspaper reporter that "Tom's out this morning working like a bird dog. He went down to the stock yards on a handshakin' expedition. Goin' to make a house-to-house canvass. . . ." [10]

Tom's political chores did not end with this door-to-door campaigning; he was given some responsibility on a higher level as well. When the Democratic party met to draw up its 1908 platform, Jim stayed at home and Tom represented the Goat faction on the resolutions committee. Also, when the Democratic City Convention met two days later, Alderman Jim was not present, but the younger Pendergast was there to represent the organization.

The Pendergast machine did not falter under Tom Pendergast's guidance, for the First Ward returned Alderman Jim to the lower house with 1330 votes to his opponent's 443. The *Kansas City Star's* pre-election statement proved to be accurate: "The First ward doesn't elect Republicans; it is immaterial who will be nominated against Pendergast. . . ." [11]

All things considered, Tom had performed well. While the entire Democratic ticket with the exception of four lower house candidates was elected, no ward in the city delivered such large majorities for the Democratic candidates as the Pendergast First. Tom Pendergast's leadership had been impressive, but it must be remembered that he had his brother's seasoned and skillful guidance behind him all of the way.

Jim Pendergast remained a power behind the scenes for another few months, while Tom Pendergast met with the Jackson County Democracy to help select the delegation for the state convention. But soon Tom Pendergast had to direct the Pendergast machine alone. With his health failing quickly, Jim Pendergast began spending much more of his time on the farm he had purchased just across the state line in Johnson County, Kansas.

The ailing alderman was too tired and too weak to carry on as the boss of the river wards, but he did find enough energy to make one last effort for the general welfare of his city. This was important because it helped remove some of the stigma that had been placed upon the name Pendergast.

Jim Pendergast is a legendary figure in Kansas City today, and one of the main reasons (aside from his aid to the poor) is because he threw his support behind the construction of a new railroad station. Kansas Citians still enjoy the Union station which was moved uptown from the West Bottoms by a vote in a special election in the autumn of 1909. Had Jim Pendergast opposed the moving of the railroad terminal, he might well have been able to rally enough votes to defeat the proposal. The moving of the station from the West Bottoms meant a decline in the property values in the area where he owned a saloon and a hotel. Likewise, the removal of the old terminal meant that railroad workers would no longer live in the Bottoms in places like the Pendergast Hotel. This meant not only a cut in Pendergast's income, it also meant that many names would be removed from the voting lists in the First Ward.

Pendergast, as he had done on other occasions, put aside his own personal interests, and wholeheartedly supported the proposal to build a new station. The construction of the new terminal was not completed until after his death. During the ceremonies celebrating the formal opening of the Union station, Thomas T. Crittenden, a former mayor, gave the late alderman these words of praise:

> Mr. Pendergast, a councilman for eighteen years, had property interests in the West Bottoms. He was not a rich man, but when he became convinced that the interest of the city as a whole demanded that the terminal move uptown, he started in and worked with all his soul for the best location for the big project.[12]

The next spring, as soon as his term in the city council expired, Alderman Jim retired from political life. No doubt his retirement saddened his large, loyal following, but his departure from politics was not as devastating to the river ward dwellers as it might have been. Jim Pendergast, as usual, had taken care of them. Before he retired, he suggested they "take Brother Tom; he'll make a fine alderman, and he'll be good to the boys just as I've been." [13] The voters took his advice, and Tom Pendergast was elected to the lower house to fill his brother's seat. Thus the underprivileged continued to receive welfare services from the Pendergast machine, services which were not readily available elsewhere prior to the coming of the New Deal.

In a few months, Alderman Jim's prolonged illness overcame him. On the night of November 10, 1911, the man who founded the Pendergast machine died. His death ended a significant era in the political history of Kansas City. As a young man, Jim Pendergast went to Kansas City and found a faction-torn, impotent Democratic party. But he soon created form and organization out of the chaos. When he died, he left his well-trained brother in control of a machine which ruled two of the largest neighborhoods in Kansas City.

Tom Pendergast was not one to squander an inheritance. He immediately embarked upon a political career during which he would not only retain the old bailiwick but expand its boundaries throughout Kansas City and rural Jackson County and into many other districts of Missouri.

It was not immediately obvious that Tom Pendergast would enhance the family's political fortunes. Indeed, some local politicians assumed that with Alderman Jim's death, the Pendergast family would fall into obscurity. One politician in Kansas City wrote to his uncle that "it is my prediction that, since Pendergast's death, Shannon will be the sole boss of this county. . . ." [14]

Perhaps the very fact that people wrote him off as ineffective gave Tom Pendergast the impetus to fight on relentlessly. In any case, the young man who had started out as a bookkeeper in Jim Pendergast's saloon quickly set his sights on expanding the riverward organization.

Alderman Jim had held the West Bottoms and North End in his

grasp by helping the poor. But Tom Pendergast had to change some of the organization's tactics in order to expand his organization. The poor and the low-income working-class citizens who inhabited the river wards could be counted on to remain loyal to the machine as long as they were cared for as they had been in the past. However, the traditional Pendergast dole of fuel, food, and clothing would not enable Tom Pendergast to organize the middle-class residential wards of the city. Similarly, other kinds of services and different approaches had to be used for the machine to expand into rural Jackson County.

4

The New Boss Expands His Domain

The Kansas City that Tom Pendergast set out to conquer was quite different from the town that Alderman Jim first organized. By 1910 the population had soared to almost 250,000, nearly five times larger than it had been when Big Jim opened his West Bottoms saloon. The city limits had expanded along with the population. Jim Pendergast spent most of his life in a Kansas City which spread southward from the Missouri River to Thirty-first Street, but by 1910 Tom hoped to organize a city that reached all the way to Seventy-ninth Street.

Kansas City had changed in many other respects too. When Alderman Jim arrived in town everyone depended upon mule-drawn streetcars for public transportation; but by the time the younger Pendergast took over the machine, Kansas City had modern trolleys. In the same vein of change, automobiles were replacing buggies. As a matter of fact, by 1910 only New York City and Chicago led Kansas City in auto sales.

Everything was up to date in Kansas City by the early 1900's. Many modern office buildings were going up in place of old frame ones. The new edifices reached unbelievable (for Kansas City) heights of seven to twelve stories, and provided as many as four hundred office spaces.

The old town's business district was undergoing some significant changes too. Not only were new buildings replacing old ones, but business sites were in ever-growing demand. Consequently, the downtown business district gradually forced the residents farther east and south. It had extended to about Ninth Street in Alderman Jim's heyday, but by 1910 it ran all the way to Twelfth Street, and even as far as Sixteenth along McGee Street. Countless houses and trees were leveled to make way for the expanding businesses. And as the arms of enterprise stretched out, the residents fled a jump or two ahead of them. The fashionable Quality Hill, for example, was deserted by most of its celebrated residents. Some of the socially elite moved several miles to the east but the majority went directly south beyond Thirty-first Street to the Old Westport district. There they built spacious stone and brick houses, many of which are standing to this day. Between the business district and these expensive, fashionable dwellings on the far south side were the modest frame houses of Kansas City's large middle class.

Tom Pendergast had his eye on the new neighborhoods that were growing up in the burgeoning city. They had to be organized before he could control the city. For all practical purposes he started directing his brother's organization toward that end in 1909. Almost immediately though, one development became noticeable. He began using illegal voting tactics, which Alderman Jim had never employed. This reflects the younger Pendergast's willingness to go to almost any lengths to increase his power and expand the machine.

When Tom Pendergast took over the machine, he started at a bad time because it was a period of weakness for the local Democrats. A Republican, Herbert S. Hadley, had entered the governor's mansion in 1909. Governor Hadley was a reformer, and his administration soon inaugurated a campaign to clear the Jackson County voter registration lists of all padding. Many names of nonresidents were dropped from lists in North End and West Bottoms wards which were controlled by Tom Pendergast. And names were also dropped from the one city ward managed by Joe Shannon.[1]

Homer Mann, one of the leading Republicans in Kansas City, attributed the sweeping Republican victory in the 1910 city election to this pruning of the voting lists.[2] But whatever the reasons for the Republican victory, the Democratic defeat meant that Tom Pendergast was faced with the problem of expanding his organization at a difficult time. Despite Pendergast's election to the aldermanic post that his brother had held since 1892, the Republicans now controlled the city government. And to make matters even worse for the Democrats, the Grand Old Party won the county elections the following fall. This meant more than a loss of elective offices to the Democrats, it meant a loss of valuable patronage.

The Goat machine was directly injured by the Republican sweep. Tom Pendergast lost the appointive office of superintendent of streets. This hurt the Pendergast organization because the superintendent handled more patronage than anyone on the city payroll save the mayor. Figures are not available for 1910, but as early as 1900, the superintendent of streets employed over two hundred men and thirty teams of horses for street work. To add to the organization's woes, Michael J. Pendergast, a brother of Tom's, lost his post as county license inspector to a Republican. This position had represented one of the first Pendergast inroads into county politics, which had been dominated primarily by Joseph B. Shannon. With the loss of the job went a combination of salary and fees amounting to approximately $3000, plus the peripheral advantage of patronage. This job also regulated the distribution of liquor and beer licenses throughout Jackson County, including all of Kansas City.

These setbacks that the Democrats received in 1910 led Tom Pendergast to form the first of several alliances that he would make with Joe Shannon. The two bosses realized that if they would pool their resources, they would have a much better chance to win the next elections from the Republicans.

When the Democratic City Convention met in the early spring of

1912 to select a ticket for the ensuing municipal election, the *Kansas City Star* reported that "'TOM' AND 'JOE' DIVIDED IT."[3] The two bosses agreed upon a mayoralty candidate, and split evenly the candidates for aldermanic seats representing each of the city's sixteen wards. Pendergast could count on the votes in the wards of the North End and West Bottoms, but to win the election the Democrats needed votes in the growing residential area in south Kansas City. Shannon could be depended upon in the Ninth Ward, but this was not enough.

Pendergast knew that his machine needed ward organizations in the expanding residential district. Thus Mike Pendergast, who became one of Tom's key lieutenants, moved into south Kansas City's middle-class Tenth Ward. He organized and incorporated the Tenth Ward Democratic Club, the first Goat residence ward organization. Tom Pendergast also had Clarence Wofford, the son of one of Alderman Jim's loyal machine politicians, working to organize the middle-class neighborhood comprising the Eighth Ward.

It was this determination which allowed Tom Pendergast, in alliance with Joe Shannon, to put the Democrats back into power in Kansas City. A Kansas City newspaper reported that "the Republicans were whipped yesterday before the polls closed. The weak, imperfect character of the Republican organization was apparent . . . even when the polls opened. . . . Opposed to the flimsy machine of the Republicans was a Democratic organization such as has not been marshalled in Kansas City for years."[4] The Democrats elected every man on the ticket who was elected at large, and they were successful in twelve of the city's sixteen wards in the contests for the council seats. Boss Tom was easily re-elected in the First Ward, and he elected his men in the Eighth and Tenth wards as well.[5]

Even though Tom Pendergast was forced to divide the patronage fifty-fifty with Shannon, things looked much brighter for his organization than they had just two years before. Pendergast now had some patronage to help fortify his new organizations in the residential wards, as well as to help him maintain his position in the old river wards. Added to this, he had recently acquired some useful prestige. In 1910 James A. Reed was elected by the Democratic-controlled state legislature to go to the United States Senate. Reed was definitely a Pendergast partisan. He had received his start in politics with the aid of Jim Pendergast, who delivered the vote which made him mayor of Kansas City in 1900. Jim Reed and Tom Pendergast became close friends, and continued to bestow political favors upon one another for years. William Reddig points out that "the Senator did not control much patronage that was useful to the Kansas City Democrats, but the prestige of his position, the power of his voice in campaigns, his advice on policy and strategy and his influence with state and national party leaders were large assets to the organization. . . ." [6]

Politically, the future looked good for Tom Pendergast after the city election in 1912. But the new leader was much more ambitious than his older brother had been; thus he was not satisfied with his position. Indeed, with things going his way, he pushed even harder for more power. The renowned Boss Plunkitt of Tammany Hall once said that when a boss wants to expand into another boss's territory "you either bide your time until he falters and dies, or you evict him, peaceably or forcibly (in the primaries) depending on your estimate of which method is better." [7] Ambitious Tom Pendergast wanted to run the county as well as the city, and he did not want to wait for Shannon to falter and die. Thus he cast aside "Fifty-Fifty," and attempted to subordinate Shannon and gain control of the county courthouse patronage.

Jackson County was not unfamiliar territory to the Pendergasts. Indeed, the machine had made a few attempts to penetrate into Shannon territory before. Thanks to these early ventures, Mike Pendergast had been the county license inspector for a time, and thereby had made a good many contacts. Mike Pendergast was no compromiser, and he did not enjoy the "Fifty-Fifty" agreement. According to one commentator who knew many of these politicians personally, "Mike consistently preached the extermination of all Rabbits." [8] Therefore he naturally relished the chore given to him

by Tom of organizing the county for the Goats as they attempted
to overthrow Joe Shannon.

The Pendergast attempt to overthrow Shannon meant more than
prestige. A Jackson County newspaper editor summed up what the
control of the county court included, citing "the big patronage
which the court holds, the big road fund, about $600,000 a year
and the revenue fund, about a million dollars a year from which
salaries are paid, and the general management of some of the
county offices. The purse strings of the county are therefore the
prize." [9] With all of this to gain, Tom felt that he had nothing to
lose by challenging Shannon at the Democratic primary in August
1912.

Wanting every advantage, the big Irishman had his ticket
printed on sample ballots and distributed by party workers before
Shannon even had his slate completed. He had all of his own
workers on the job, as well as Jim Reed's prestige and personal
employees at work for him.[10] But Pendergast was not overcon-
fident, for he did not underestimate Shannon's strength in Jackson
County. Thus, he enlisted the aid of Thomas R. Marks, one of the
two major faction leaders in the local Republican party. This was
the first occasion, but not the last, that Tom Pendergast made a
deal with Republican boss Marks to get Republican voters on his
side in Democratic primary contests. Although this was illegal,
Pendergast found it quite helpful. Robert "Bob" Hawkins, a Pendergast lieutenant, served as one of the contact men for this
alliance. Hawkins was a 300-pounder who always carried a cane
and sported an unlighted cigar. He established his reputation as
the organization's liaison man with the Republican faction of Tom
Marks.

Pendergast's determination, hard work, and alliance with Marks,
produced the desired results on election day. The *Kansas City Star*
reported that "an analysis of the vote shows that the Pendergast
machine was well oiled and carried every office on the slate except
prosecuting attorney and congressman from the Fifth District." [11]
It was an important victory for Pendergast who had demonstrated

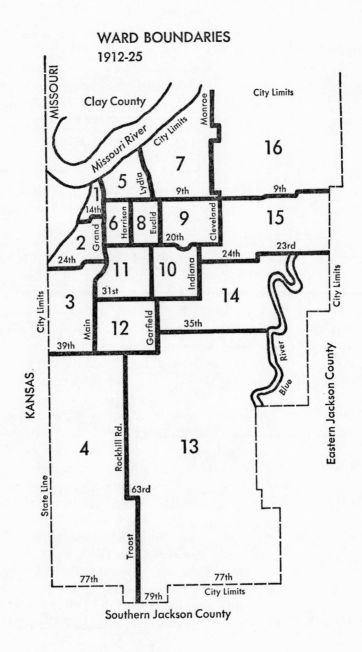

WARD BOUNDARIES
1912-25

beyond a doubt that he was the major power in the county, as well as in Kansas City. He likewise elected twenty-nine of the forty-one members of the county committee, which gave him a controlling majority. The control of the county committee was important, for it was that body which selected the Fifth District members to the state committee.

Although the election was a significant victory for Pendergast, it was not devastating to Shannon. Even though most Pendergast candidates won nomination, the election returns showed that the majorities were not overwhelming. The very fact that two Shannon men were nominated for important positions proved that Shannon still had strength in the county. It was this fact, plus Pendergast's realization that the nomination of his candidates did not mean automatic Democratic victory in November, that led him to offer concessions to the Rabbit boss in return for November support of the ticket. Pendergast's organization could have selected both members to the state committee, because the Goats controlled the county committee. But Pendergast allowed Shannon to accompany him as the second state committeeman from the Fifth District.

Practicality forced Pendergast to compromise with Shannon again, rather than risk defeat of his ticket in the general election in November. The alliance of necessity for both faction leaders helped produce a Democratic victory. The entire Democratic county slate was elected. Even though Tom Pendergast was forced to share the spoils of victory with his enemy, he was in a stronger position than ever before. He now had R. D. Mize, one of his own men, elected as a county judge. While there were still two other judges who could overrule Mize on any issue, they were not partisans of either faction. But Pendergast at least had one man in the top decision-making office of the county. While Pendergast could not have done it alone, he was obviously the strongest faction leader in Kansas City and Jackson County. He was not going unrecognized, for in just a few months Ralph Lozier, a Democrat from halfway across the state in the Second District, called upon him. Lozier asked Pendergast to urge President Woodrow Wilson to appoint him to a post in the diplomatic service.[12] While Pendergast may not have had any influence in Washington at this time, he did before the year was out. Frank Walsh, a Kansas City lawyer, was appointed by President Wilson in 1913 to head the Industrial Relations Commission. Walsh later remembered that he honored Tom Pendergast's requests for patronage every time he could possibly do so.[13]

Tom Pendergast's expanding organization had helped get his men elected in the city and county. Thus there was more patronage than before from the city and county, and there was even a dribble coming from at least one source in Washington. In order to maintain the loyalty of his workers, and entice more, the big Irishman had to reward his followers. One Kansas City politician understood why Tom was gaining such a large following of workers: "Pendergast has taken care of his workers," he asserted.[14] But the Pendergast brothers were doing more than that. While the loyal workers in the party were taken care of, the constituents were not forgotten either. A Roman Catholic priest, commenting on Mike Pendergast, said, "We have known him for twenty-seven years and never in that time have we gone to him in vain for aid for a needy person." [15] And a typical comment about Tom Pendergast, from his days as Alderman Jim's ward heeler to the end of his reign, was that "he pays hundreds of dollars a year in room rents, dinners and the like just to keep the voters in his grasp." [16]

The question immediately arises, how did Pendergast get the money to provide such services to his growing constituency? The boss did own the Pendergast Wholesale Liquor Company, and he owned a third-rate house called the Jefferson Hotel. He probably made an adequate income from these investments, but it is difficult to believe that he made enough to finance the extensive welfare program that he carried on continuously. Undoubtedly his legitimate income was bolstered by a "cut" that he surely received from the prostitution that thrived in his hotel. What was going on there was no secret. One Kansas City Democrat referred to the Jefferson Hotel crowd as "the pimp and whore element." [17]

Likewise, Pendergast took advantage of other extra-legal opportunities to make money. He certainly wanted some of the money for himself, but also needed it for his machine. Indeed, in 1914, a rare opportunity arose which offered the Goat leader a chance to earn some money and gain the friendship and support of some influential businessmen and politicians.

The Metropolitan Street Railway Company in Kansas City wanted to obtain a new thirty-year franchise from the city. The franchise that it held at the time was eleven years from expiration. According to the *Kansas City Star*, the "Met," as it was known in the city, wanted the new franchise because it was in financial trouble. The new franchise would ease this situation because under the new terms street-car rates would be increased and the company's taxes to the city would be reduced by approximately $157,000 annually. The "Met" argued that many citizens who lived in new neighborhoods that had grown up since the days of the old franchise were demanding services extended to them and that they deserved them. But to do so would necessitate the new franchise.[18]

The proposed franchise was submitted to the voters in a special election in the summer of 1914. This franchise, which the *Star* considered a bad investment for the citizens of Kansas City, won by less than 7000 votes with almost 40,000 cast. The franchise, the *Star* accused, would never have passed had it not been for the large votes cast for it in the North Side wards. The article went on to say that the huge majorities in those wards could never have been produced if it had not been for the use of repeat voters, money, and strong-arm tactics. It was argued that the "Met" spent thousands of dollars, hoping to gain millions.[19] A *Kansas City Times* article pointed out that the Pendergast machine worked hand-in-hand with the Republicans in putting the franchise over on the people.[20]

Scores of witnesses in court several months later testified that Tom Pendergast did work with the Republicans, and used money, repeat voters, and toughs to produce North Side majorities that pushed the franchise to victory. The night before the election, he held a meeting at the Jefferson Hotel to put the finishing touches on the organization he was preparing for the franchise election. About three hundred men were on hand to consume liquor and cigars that were handed out with the electioneering instructions. Tom Pendergast was aided by Tom Marks, the Republican politician whom he had just recently called to his aid in the primary election. Conrad Mann, a leading member of the Republican party, general manager of the Kansas City Breweries Company, and future president of the chamber of commerce, was there too. Harry Sandler, owner of a local cement company and personal friend of big Tom's, was also there to aid the franchise cause.[21]

Election day brought an unusually large turnout for a special election. In fact, 74.3 per cent of those who were registered voted. One of the major reasons why so many voters went to the polls was because an unprecedented drive was staged by the most influential politicians in the city to get them there. Witnesses under oath testified that Cas Welch, a white ward boss in the Negro neighborhoods, had a large group of Negro ward heelers out buying drinks and giving money to voters. Joe Shannon and Tom Pendergast were giving a hand too. Conrad Mann was seen delivering bags of money to Homer Mann, a leading member of the local Republican party. And some of Pendergast's Italian lieutenants were buying drinks and passing out silver dollars to encourage men to vote for the franchise. Members of his organization paid men to vote under assumed names; and election judges who questioned some of those dragged off the streets and out of flop houses to vote were intimidated and abused, both verbally and physically.[22]

To the Metropolitan Street Railway Company, these illegal tactics were worth what they cost. In some of the Pendergast controlled precincts, the vote was unbelievably favorable. One precinct, for example, produced 258 votes for the new franchise, and only one against it. And in another Pendergast precinct, only four votes were cast in opposition to the wishes of the "Met."

What was clearly a defeat for urban democracy was a victory

for Tom Pendergast. It would be naïve to assume that he did not receive some remuneration from the Metropolitan Street Railway Company for spearheading such a splendid performance for them. But far more than a financial gain was made in the summer of 1914 by the Goat chieftain. This election had strengthened his alliance with the Republican boss, Tom Marks, who would work with Pendergast again for jobs or other rewards. Pendergast also gained the assistance of a rising young Democratic boss in Ward Two, Miles Bulger. Bulger controlled a low- to middle-income neighborhood which was undergoing a transition from a residential area to a retail district. Pendergast had not organized the Second Ward, and he and Bulger would work together again. Pendergast also ingratiated himself with an important businessman and Republican party leader, Conrad Mann. This relationship would last for years to come. Mann would one day be able to help the Pendergast machine, and Boss Pendergast, in turn, would perform some useful services for Mann.

It is clear that in just a few years, Tom Pendergast had succeeded in expanding the organization into areas where Alderman Jim had never carried it; but he had used some illegal tactics that the old boss had never employed. By 1914 Tom Pendergast had built ward organizations in some of the middle-class, residential districts, he had consummated some working agreements with Tom Marks and Miles Bulger, and he had made some important contacts in the business community.

Pendergast was obviously coming to the front as a powerful boss in the metropolitan area. He had gained control of the Democratic City Central Committee in the spring of 1914, and his organization led the party to a victory in the city election which meant two more years of domination in the city government. The man who had been shrugged off as a "heavy-jowled oaf"—the man whose faction was believed destined for oblivion with the death of its founder—had demonstrated in four years' time that he was a power not to be ignored.

5

The Campaign To Dominate
the Local Democratic Party and
the County Government

Before Tom Pendergast could realize his goal of dominating the governments of Kansas City and rural Jackson County, he first had to become the recognized boss of the local Democratic party. By 1914 the rising boss was actually nothing more than the leader of a growing faction. Although his organization was already becoming the strongest in the Missouri Democratic party, he wanted to make it so strong that he could command the support of other faction leaders and ward bosses on his own terms. In other words, he wanted to be able to deliver so many votes through his own organization's efforts that he would not be dependent upon any single faction leader or ward boss. In this way then, the other leaders would have to come to him. They would offer to deliver their votes on election day, but the spoils would be divided on Tom Pendergast's terms.

For example, in the city elections of 1912 and 1914 Tom Pendergast was forced to make a fifty-fifty agreement with Joe Shannon. By itself the Goat faction could not have won the elections. Pendergast's machine could not deliver enough votes to win the city-wide election without the support of Shannon's block of votes.

Under such conditions Pendergast devised a plan to subordinate all significant faction leaders in Kansas City to his machine.

There were three leaders with whom Pendergast had to contend. Shannon, of course, was his biggest problem but there were also Miles Bulger and Casimir J. Welch. As we have seen, Bulger was the boss of Ward Two which bordered the North Side wards. Known to Kansas City politicians as the "Little Czar," Bulger was an independent, skillful organizer who was elected to the lower house from his ward in 1912 and 1914. Cas Welch was a municipal judge who was re-elected many times from the Sixth District, which he controlled. This district was comprised of sections of Ward Six and Ward Eight in the central part of the city, and Welch had an efficient machine which he proudly referred to as "Little Tammany." [1] There were many Negroes in Welch's district, and he gained most of his support from them.

Tom Pendergast did not waste any time in his effort to become the head of the local Democracy. In the Democratic primary in 1914, he made a deal with Miles Bulger. Pendergast agreed to support Bulger for the nomination to a spot on the three-man county court if Bulger in turn would back Judge R. D. Mize for another term. Mize was Pendergast's only man on the county court. If he could get one more man elected, the machine would be able to control the lucrative county administration. Pendergast joined hands with Bulger in hopes of preventing Shannon from nominating his men to dominate the court.

Pendergast and Bulger did not spare any effort in their attempt to defeat Shannon's candidate in the primary. They put their own ward organizations into action, but they also went on a hand-shaking expedition out in the county. A rural newspaper pointed out that the farmers generally did not differentiate between Rabbits and Goats and were not particularly in favor of either faction. What they actually wanted was a country man who would take care of the rural interests.[2] But Pendergast and his ally had one big point in their favor. Judge Mize, whom the Goats had sponsored two years before, had turned out to be an excellent judge.

The Independence *Examiner* conceded that even those who had opposed Mize must admit he had done a great deal for the country districts. "More road contracts," the editor observed, "have been let and more miles of road built than in any other term since roads became the issue in Jackson County." [3]

Judge Mize's reputation undoubtedly aided the Pendergast slate, but so did the organization's effort in the city wards. The machine delivered an enormous block of votes from its own wards, and it even had a group of workers laboring in Shannon territory to offset some of his strength. Pendergast's effort was successful, for Mize and Bulger both won.

The *Kansas City Star* reported that "as a result of yesterday's primary, Joe Shannon becomes a second-rate power in Jackson County." [4] The statement was perhaps a bit premature, but the handwriting was on the wall. Shannon did support the ticket in its November victory and for his support was given some patronage. But it was on Boss Tom's terms, said a reporter, and it amounted to only a few "crumbs." [5]

If Pendergast could keep Shannon on the defensive for a while longer, he would be well on his way to obtaining some of the patronage that a Democratic governor could offer to a local leader. The Board of Police Commissioners in Kansas City controlled the police force. The governor appointed the members of this board, and at this particular time Shannon men were in power. Tom Pendergast intended to wrest this plum from Shannon, and he succeeded in a masterful way.

Pendergast realized that if he could demonstrate beyond a doubt that he could control the Democratic party in the city just as he had done in the county, his machine would receive the Kansas City patronage from the Democratic governor of Missouri, Elliott W. Major. The first step Pendergast made in gaining the Governor's respect was to dictate the selection of delegates from Jackson County to the Democratic State Convention at St. Joseph. A Kansas City newspaper pointed out that Governor Major wanted to be Vice President, "but he needs something besides Shannon support in the state convention. He must have Pendergast support from Jackson County if he gets any help, as Pendergast snowed Shannon under so far yesterday in the election that Shannon won't be a factor." [6] The results of the contests for the Jackson County delegation to the state convention already had the governor wondering if he had made an error in 1913 by giving all of the police and election commissioner patronage to Shannon.

It did not take the governor long to realize that he had bet on the wrong man in 1913. When the delegates from Jackson County arrived in St. Joseph, the defeated Shannon was not there. But Tom Pendergast was on hand, with a host of noisy delegates who were endorsing Governor Major and supporting his vice presidential boom. The Pendergast crowd made a lasting impression. The *Star* reported that

> "The goat special" over the Kansas City, Clay County & St. Joseph trolley line got in at 10 o'clock, bearing about five hundred stalwart Pendergast men. In all there were five carloads. Every man wore a button. Its only inscription was one without words, a picture of a goat rampant.[7]

And in case that was not enough to remind Missouri Democrats which faction was running Jackson County, the Pendergast boys brought along a live goat as their mascot. The day after the convention it was obvious that Governor Major had realized his mistake. He made peace with Pendergast. Shannon's domination of gubernatorial patronage in Kansas City and Jackson County would soon come to an end.

Shannon was sinking fast, but he was not going to concede without a fight. If he could produce a show of strength at the city election, he might still warrant some recognition. In the city convention the Rabbit chieftain demanded the renomination of Mayor Henry Jost. With almost no hesitation, Pendergast marched out of the meeting and decided to prove that no Democrat could win in Kansas City without his support. Shannon accepted the challenge, undoubtedly realizing full well that if he lost now, on top of his other recent defeats at the hands of Pendergast, he would never again be recognized as a power in local politics. Leading Democrats were disturbed about the split in the local Democracy. Senator James A. Reed, for example, made a speech to urge the two faction leaders to bury the hatchet.

Pendergast ignored Reed's pleas. Instead, he backed the Republican mayoralty candidate, and supported a handful of "Independent" candidates for alderman. The "Independent" candidates included John P. O'Neil in Pendergast's place from Ward One, and Pendergast's new ally Miles Bulger from Ward Two. At the same time Pendergast started a voter registration drive. At one point his workers bragged that they were registering four men to every one that Shannon's men were placing on the books. In six precincts of Ward One alone, the Pendergast organization added 1163 names to the registration list, but the Shannons failed to register many new voters.[8]

The Pendergast machine was functioning smoothly. Thanks to its insistence that a union label be carried on all city and county supplies, the local American Federation of Labor backed Bulger wholeheartedly.[9] As always, Pendergast had his chief lieutenant in the First Ward, Charles Clark, getting out the vote. In the area known as "Little Italy," Pendergast had Mike Ross on the job. Ross was an Irishman, but he had a group of young Italian men, like Johnny Lazia, working for him at the grass roots level. It is significant that Pendergast, attempting to defeat Shannon, helped elect a Republican, George H. Edwards, who pledged a reform government for Kansas City. Edwards's was also supported by Missouri's ex-governor, the progressive Herbert S. Hadley. Reformer Hadley made speeches urging the defeat of Shannon's candidate Jost, who stood for "reaction" and "corruption." [10]

Shannon must have sensed his defeat. In a last desperate attempt to win the election, he made use of the police force for the last time before its control was turned over to Pendergast. Before sunrise on election morning, the police herded literally hundreds of Pendergast supporters from North End bunkhouses to the police station for "investigation," and refused to honor writs of habeas corpus issued to free 311 captives. Such disregard for the law sent the acting chief of police to jail. According to the *Kansas City Star,* by 6 o'clock on the morning of the election, "two hundred Pendergast men had been arrested by the Shannonized police department. The patrol wagons had been running in pairs since 3 o'clock." [11] But Shannon was not able to do much damage, even with his misuse of the city police. When the election returns were tallied, his mayoralty candidate carried only two wards. Edwards won an overwhelming victory, with his largest majorities coming from the Pendergast strongholds. According to Shannon's political biographer, this municipal election of 1916 was "the most important defeat of Shannon's career." [12]

The fact that Shannon was no longer a power in local politics was pointed out once more a few weeks later, after the Democratic primaries in Jackson County. One newspaper put the point across with a front page cartoon showing a goat butting a rabbit over a fence and out of a cabbage patch. According to the Independence *Examiner,* Shannon recognized he was defeated, and thus he "submitted" to Pendergast control at the meeting of the County Central Committee. In the final analysis, it was a good year for Boss Pendergast. Having crushed the opposition of the once powerful Joe Shannon, Pendergast, at the helm of the Democratic party, elected its entire ticket in Jackson County the following November. The pluralities, reported a county newspaper, "in some cases ran into several thousands." [13]

Once Pendergast reached this position of power in 1916, he immediately utilized it to his own advantage, and to the advantage of some other groups in the community. The boss's newly acquired control of the police department was quickly used to aid Kansas City prostitutes. Pendergast informed the city's policemen that if there was any molestation of his "friends," those responsible would join the ranks of the unemployed.[14]

Pendergast also used the patronage that he received from Governor Frederick D. Gardner in 1917 to protect the liquor interests which were spread throughout the city and county. Excise commissioners were appointed by Gardner at Pendergast's suggestion.[15] With Mike Pendergast recently appointed license inspector again, and Goats entrenched in all of the commissioner posts, Pendergast could easily bestow favors upon select businessmen.

Not only the liquor interests and prostitutes, but also favored contractors were aided. The Ross Construction Company, in which Tom Pendergast eventually became a partner, received special consideration on county road contracts from the court over which Miles Bulger presided with Pendergast's blessings.[16] It is significant too, that the owner of the company was Mike Ross, who was Pendergast's lieutenant in Ward Five.

The existing evidence suggests that the gambling interests were being served by Boss Pendergast too. Local gambling had been protected by Alderman Jim when he controlled the police force, so it is likely that Tom Pendergast was sympathetic to it. Indeed, on election days the North Side wards were always loaded with Pendergast workers who were known to be a part of the gambling interests in Kansas City and Jackson County. In the city election in 1918, for example, Jim Pryor, Booth Baughman, and Phil Mc-Crory all worked for the Goat machine. All three of these ward heelers had been a part of the gambling and saloon combine since the days of Alderman Jim.

Pendergast also continued to help the indigent. Christmas dinners were provided every year, and handouts of food, fuel, and clothing were provided by the machine the year around. Thus it is easy to see why the votes kept coming in from underprivileged citizens in the North Side wards, while Pendergast was busily working to expand his machine.

The fact that Pendergast had made himself the most powerful Democrat in the city and county did not mean that he held this position unchallenged. Actually, he had some hurdles to overcome before he became so thoroughly established that his opposition became insignificant.

One of the challenges came from within the Democratic party.

The sudden emergence of the challenge was a surprise because it had appeared that the different factions finally were able to work together in Jackson County. In the 1918 election, for example, Shannon, Bulger, and Pendergast worked together. By backing one of Shannon's friends for a major office, Pendergast was able to get Shannon to support Bulger for re-election. Bulger needed all the help he could get, because his shabby record on road contracts[17] made him a weak candidate; but he did not appreciate the aid that he had received. He rebelled against his subordination to Pendergast and attempted to use his patronage power as presiding judge to force the county organization to recognize him as the boss of the county rather than Tom Pendergast.

Bulger's visions of grandeur were smashed by the primary election in the late summer of 1920. Pendergast was forced to make a fifty-fifty deal with Shannon to gain his support, and that was quite a concession since Shannon's strength did not match Pendergast's. However, Pendergast was faced with an attack on his county organization, and he was therefore more than willing to satisfy his old rival's demands.

The Goats did not neglect anything in their determination to crush Bulger's bid to get his own ticket nominated. Tom Pendergast not only made certain that he would have Rabbit support, but he also bargained to renew his working agreement with Tom Marks, the Republican boss. By offering patronage to the job-hungry Republican ward leaders, Pendergast was able to get the extra-legal support of some Republican voters who lived in the river wards.[18]

Pendergast, in alliance with Shannon and the so-called "Boss Republicans," defeated Bulger's ticket in the 1920 primary. But a more formidable threat awaited the boss in the coming general election. The Democratic party under Pendergast's guidance had acquired an extremely bad image, and the Republican party made the most of it. In the year when the national Republican leadership was calling for a return to "normalcy," the Missouri Republicans called for removal of the corruption in state and local government.

Much of their criticism was centered on Pendergast, who had used the police force in the previous city election. Governor Frederick Gardner in 1920, and his predecessor Elliot Major, were Democrats who gave Pendergast control of the police department. In the spring of 1920, the city election took place under deplorable conditions. The Pendergast-dominated police stood by in silence as Rabbits and Goats used repeat voters and thugs to produce large enough majorities in several wards to win the election.[19]

These events alone made many people look upon the Democratic party with suspicion. However, there was more criticism to come. The county court under Democratic rule was under attack by the newspapers for excessive spending and questionable contracting.

The Republican candidate for governor, Arthur M. Hyde, promised that if he were elected an immediate end would be put to the Pendergast- and Shannon-controlled police department. He argued that he would appoint a board of police commissioners which would not tolerate the election stealing permitted by the Democratic party.[20]

Missourians were ready for a change and in November they elected Hyde governor and other Republicans to most of the county offices. Only one Democrat managed to win election to the county court. Thus with Bulger a holdover on the court for two more years, and a Republican newly elected to it, Pendergast lost control of the three-man county court.

This successful challenge to his power in Jackson County forced Pendergast to rethink his position and change his strategy. The boss decided that patronage from the county court was essential to his machine. He needed a man who could win a county judgeship in rural Jackson County despite its antagonism to him and to the inefficient and corrupt court which he had controlled.

Desperately wanting to regain and maintain the rich county patronage, Tom Pendergast decided that he would be willing to relinquish, if necessary, such assets to his machine as special favors to contractors. This is exactly what Pendergast had to do when he

selected Harry Truman to become the machine's candidate for
county judge. Truman was selected to run for eastern district judge
for several reasons. First of all, James M. Pendergast, Mike's son,
was becoming very active in politics. He had served in World
War I with Truman, and he suggested him to his father as a possibility. Not only did young Pendergast know and trust Truman,
but the latter had some important assets. He was well known
throughout the county because he had lived there since he was a
small boy, had relatives scattered throughout the rural precincts,
and was a Baptist, a Legionnaire, and a Mason. Moreover, Truman
did not have the taint of being a city politician eager to tell the
country boys what was best for their district. [21]

Truman won the nomination in August 1922 and then went on to
victory in November. The day that he was elected was an important turning point for the Pendergast machine in Jackson County.
Corruption ceased in the court with Truman's victory, but Pendergast's domination of the county administration continued until
the machine collapsed in 1939. Truman did lose when he ran for
re-election in 1924, but that was due to a tactical error on the part
of the Pendergast machine. Shannon had helped elect Truman in
1922, but Truman and the other Goats on the court cut off the
Rabbits with almost no patronage.[22] Thus Shannon's refusal to
support Truman in 1924 cost the Democrats just enough votes to
cause him to fall victim to his Republican opponent. At some other
election the Pendergast faction could have done without Shannon's
support, but the Coolidge landslide brought so many votes to Republican candidates that the Democrats needed every vote they
could muster.

Truman ran again in 1926, this time for presiding judge. He won,
and became so important to the machine that when Mike Pendergast died in 1929, Truman took over the leadership of the county
organization.[23] However, he refused to favor the contractors who
were friends of the machine and had been given special treatment
by Miles Bulger. No company was awarded a contract to do
county work unless it was the lowest bidder. This included the

new company which Pendergast himself had recently started—the
Ready-Mixed Concrete Company. In 1928, for example, when
Truman was successful in getting a $6,500,000 road building pro-
gram adopted by the voters, 225 miles of road were paved and
of the total the Ready-Mixed Concrete Company paved only
three-fourths of a mile.[24]

Truman would not deal in graft, but he was successful in
running the Pendergast machine in rural Jackson County because
he was an astute organizer who used patronage to the organization's advantage. In addition, Truman managed the court so
efficiently, and accomplished so much while in office, that he won
a large following. The *Kansas City Star,* for example, never supported Pendergast candidates, and neither did the *Examiner,*
which was published in Independence. Both papers, however,
praised Truman's record and gave him their editorial support each
time he ran for the county court.

Another Truman booster was Walter Matscheck. The epitome of
the pre-World War I progressives, Matscheck always campaigned
for the judge. Matscheck had studied under Richard T. Ely at
Wisconsin and he later came to Kansas City to organize and head
the Civic Research Institute. The organization was financed by a
number of civic leaders who were dedicated to the belief that
"democratic government can be efficient." The Civic Research Institute studied local government and made suggestions for improvement. Matscheck often found himself at loggerheads with
Pendergast, but he had nothing but praise for Truman. The reformer found especially praiseworthy Truman's plan to reorganize
the court for increased efficiency.[25]

Judge Truman worked hard to build an efficient county government that would be free of the corruption and waste of the Bulger
days. Indeed, the future President of the United States, in his
typical blunt and straightforward manner, volunteered to have his
court investigated by a grand jury. He offered to appear before a
grand jury himself, and he said, "I am inviting the closest investigation, because I am proud of the record of the County Court."[26]

By leaving Truman alone to manage the county administration as he saw fit, Pendergast lost the graft which he had bestowed upon his associates during the Bulger regime.[27] However, by letting Truman have his way, the Pendergast machine controlled the patronage of the county court for a long time because Truman's excellent reputation allowed the Goats to remain in power.

Thus, by curbing his greediness, Tom Pendergast successfully overcame the 1920 challenge which had threatened to destroy his power in Jackson County. By endorsing honest government and settling for patronage alone, he had entrenched his machine in the county administration by the mid-1920's.

At almost the same time that Truman was establishing himself on the county level, Tom Pendergast became recognized as the leader of the Kansas City Democracy. This was especially evident when Cas Welch, the independent boss who had almost always sided with Shannon in Rabbit and Goat quarrels, joined Pendergast in the mid-1920's. Likewise, some of Shannon's own lieutenants saw where power lay. They deserted Shannon and threw their lot in with Boss Tom. All of those who joined the Pendergast organization from Shannon's ranks were helpful, but the greatest addition to the machine was James P. Aylward.

Jim Aylward was a well-known Kansas City lawyer. He had a large following in the city and county, and he had been chairman of the Democratic County Committee when Fifty-Fifty had been worked out between the bosses. Aylward was destined soon to become Tom Pendergast's right-hand man and chief organizer for the city, county, and state.

In 1914 Tom Pendergast had begun his plan to put himself at the head of the Democratic party in Kansas City and Jackson County. By the mid-'twenties he had achieved that objective, thanks to his selection of Harry Truman to run the county court, to the recruitment of Jim Aylward, and to the annexation of Cas Welch's "Little Tammany."

The new leader had no sooner fulfilled his ambition to control the county government than he found himself facing a serious challenge in Kansas City. If he were to maintain his machine's hold on the city government, he needed to act quickly and effectively. In 1925 the Progressive movement was far from dead in Kansas City. Having worked tirelessly for months, the reformers organized a campaign to free the city, in their words, from "boss rule." But the boss, especially now that he had the help of Welch and Aylward, proved difficult to remove.

6

Supremacy in Kansas City

Tom Pendergast was the leader of the local Democracy by 1925, but his position in Kansas City was not unchallenged. His machine was tested in Kansas City during the years of Republican strength that followed the First World War. Pendergast led the Democrats to victory in 1920, but his success was largely due to repeat voters and strong-arm tactics that would have made Boss Tweed envious.[1] In 1922, however, the Republicans themselves admitted that the city election was the most honest one held there in years. This was because the new police commissioner did not allow wholesale election stealing to take place while the police stood idly by. However, despite the fact that the police force had been taken away from Pendergast, the Democrats were victorious. The local Republican leaders frankly admitted that the Democrats won because they had won the support of the women voters, and that they had succeeded in enticing the Negroes away from the party of Lincoln.[2]

Nevertheless, Pendergast was unable to win the city election two years later. This was due to a temporary split in the local Democratic party, and to the improvement of the Republican organization. To make matters even worse for the Democratic

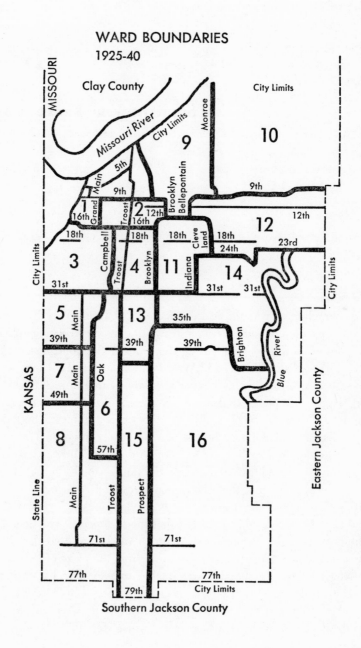

WARD BOUNDARIES
1925-40

Clay County

MISSOURI

Missouri River

City Limits

Clay County

City Limits

Monroe

9

10

5th

Main

9th

Brooklyn

Bellepontain

9th

1

Grand

16th

Troost

2

12th

16th

12th

18th

Campbell

Troost

18th

18th

Cleveland

18th

12

3

4

Brooklyn

11

Indiana

24th

23rd

City Limits

31st

31st

14

31st

31st

City Limits

5

Main

13

35th

Brighton

Blue

River

Eastern Jackson County

39th

39th

39th

7

Main

Oak

49th

KANSAS

6

57th

8

15

16

State Line

Main

Troost

Prospect

71st

71st

77th

77th

City Limits

79th

Southern Jackson County

organization, a reform movement was being organized at the same time. The reformers were sponsoring a new city charter designed to inaugurate a nonpartisan government in Kansas City. The charter movement was led by Walter Matscheck, director of the Kansas City Civic Research Institute, and R. E. McDonnell, leader of the Charter League. McDonnell, the head of a prominent engineering firm in Kansas City, had been active in the charter reform movements for several years. He and Matscheck worked untiringly and received the support of many business and professional men, ministers, educators, and women active in various civic clubs. The *Kansas City Star* also backed the movement—it could always be counted on to support a movement which promised to curb Boss Pendergast's power. Likewise, the managers of the anti-boss faction of the Republican party jumped on the bandwagon for obvious reasons.

The most articulate Republican spokesman for the "Nonpartisan" charter was Mayor Albert I. Beach who had been elected just a few months before, in the 1924 city election. In his early forties, Beach, who had been a member of both houses of the Common Council, added prestige to the movement. His administration was quite popular, and he was expected to run for re-election if the charter was adopted.

Pendergast faced a challenge not only to his supremacy in the city but to his control of the party machinery as well. For no matter how powerful he might become on the county level, he would not be able to maintain his leadership of the party very long, or preserve or expand his organization, without the spoils of office in Kansas City. And the new charter movement, on its face, appeared to be a serious threat. It was a direct attack on everything that Pendergast needed to maintain his power. Imbued with idealism, the reformers had drafted a charter which promised, if adopted, to give Kansas City an honest, efficient, nonpartisan city administration. The charter called for dividing the city's sixteen wards into four districts. A nonpartisan election would be held every four years. The mayor and four councilmen would be elected at large, and four councilmen would be elected from each of the four districts. The government would be the council-manager form, and theoretically the allotment and expenditure of municipal funds would be handled in the most open fashion. According to a study of the charter and the first twenty-five years of its operation,

> . . . reports on the state of the funds were to be required from every department to manager, council, and public. Another important theme in the new system concerned the problem of personnel: all department heads, as well as the city manager, were to be men of special training in their fields, and were to be appointed on a nonpartisan basis.[3]

Matscheck viewed the situation this way:

> . . . the point is that the real business of government, particularly local government—the unit of the city—is not governing in any strict sense. It is administering. It is doing work, carrying on operations like street cleaning, building sewers, putting out fires, and so on. That's not a matter of political science, not of governing in the older sense. It's administrative science, and that's where democracy is working. The cities that have adopted the manager form of administration are showing the state and federal governments how democracy can be made to work freed from the political machinery that has been built up around them.[4]

This was the municipal reformers' panacea. Inefficiency, graft, corruption, and the spoils system would be destroyed by the new charter, and Boss Tom Pendergast and his kind would be no more. But as has often been the case, the municipal reformers were long on idealism and short on political acumen.

One of Pendergast's judges on the county court pointed out that the boss realized that the majority of the citizens were behind the new charter.[5] Therefore, if he hoped to make himself the boss of Kansas City, it would be extremely unwise to oppose what the majority of the community wanted. Thus, to the dismay of the reformers, Pendergast pledged his support to the proposal at the last minute. His new allies, Cas Welch and Jim Aylward, labored with him, and they helped the machine deliver big majorities for the charter. Only Joe Shannon, with the remnants of his organization, fought the proposal. On February 24, 1925, Kansas Citians turned out to vote the proposed charter into law. The new charter passed by a solid majority, and carried every ward but Joe Shannon's Ninth.

What did Pendergast gain from this? In a few months, he became the most powerful man in Kansas City. The first mayor and councilmen under the new charter were to be elected for a four-year term in November 1925. All that the Pendergast machine had to do was elect five of the nine members of the council—the mayor was the ninth member, ex officio. As A. Theodore Brown pointed out, if the machine could elect five of the nine members, "its political prospects were limitless, especially so because it would then have the power to select the city manager." [6] So Pendergast's task was laid out before him. If he won, he would become one of the nation's most powerful bosses. If he lost, he would be without a voice in the city administration for the next four years.

According to the new charter, a primary election would be held with no party labels attached to the candidates' names. The two candidates for each office with the most votes would be placed on the nonpartisan ballot in the general election. But the whole concept of nonpartisanship was already a sham in the first campaign. The existing Republican and Democratic party machinery swung into action because no alternatives had been devised. The Democrats held a caucus at the Kansas City Athletic Club and elected a slate. The meeting was dominated by the Pendergast faction. Not a single Rabbit was placed on the ticket. Ben Jaudon, a Goat who had made a good record as city comptroller for many years, was selected to head the ticket. The Republicans held a caucus too, and gave the top post to Albert Beach, the Republican mayor of Kansas City. The so-called "Beach" and "Jaudon" tickets, known to everyone as the Republicans and Democrats respectively, easily won the right in the primary to appear on the ballot in the November election.

The formalities were over, and now the real battle started. Tom Pendergast put everything he had into the campaign. He had his usual band of workers prepare the North Side wards for the election, but a problem arose there which undoubtedly worried him. The governor was S. A. Baker, a Republican, and therefore, the Board of Election Commissioners was not at Pendergast's beck and call. Just prior to the election over 6000 names were struck from the registration lists in wards One, Two, Five, Six, and Eight—all Pendergast strongholds. Although the wards would still be solidly behind the machine's ticket, the huge majority from that part of the city would be reduced significantly.

Pendergast, though, was by no means devastated. He could rely on a sizable vote from the West Bottoms and North End regardless, and he was working hard to win votes in the residential wards. Mike Pendergast and his son Jim had built an efficient organization in the residential Tenth Ward, and Shannon had agreed to a compromise and would deliver his residential Ninth Ward. Pendergast also held large rallies in the residential wards, featuring such eloquent speakers as Senator James A. Reed. C. Jasper Bell, a young attorney who was trying to organize some of the middle-class neighborhoods, campaigned for Ben Jaudon in a way that would appeal to such people. He argued that Jaudon would adhere to "the principles of business administration as set out in the new charter." [7] In addition, the wife of a prominent Kansas City lawyer, Mrs. Henry N. Ess, headed a women's committee which worked many hours for the Pendergast ticket. [8]

The election was so close that the results were not known for several days. When the official tallies were made it was a happy day for the Democratic party and its boss. Mayor Beach, the Republican, was re-elected by only 428 votes out of more than 114,000 cast. But the Democrats (all Goats), won five of the seats on the city council. There could be no valid argument that the police or election commissioners stole it for Boss Tom, because they were not under his thumb anymore. Moreover, Pendergast argued that an honest election would have given Ben Jaudon the mayoralty victory. He demanded a recount and said "we want those ballot boxes opened. A contest will be a costly thing, but the pride of the Democracy is aroused." [9]

There was no recount, and although Tom Pendergast probably thought the count was accurate anyway, his language was quite significant. It might have appeared somewhat incongruous for the ex-ward heeler to speak so righteously. However, this was just the beginning of a new look. Pendergast had backed a reform charter; he was now posing as the guardian of honest elections, and he would very soon become a spokesman for efficient city government conducted on sound business principles. The boss's role had changed. He was no longer a ward heeler—he was now the head of his party and boss of his city. With his changed role was to come a new image.

Undoubtedly, Tom Pendergast wanted to change his image because he desired the increased status that went along with it. Indeed, a few years earlier he had moved out of the West Bottoms to a residential neighborhood. And in a short time he would build a $175,000 house in one of the most exclusive sections of Kansas City. But there was more to all of this than mere middle-class drive and status-seeking. Pendergast was power-hungry, and he still had not fulfilled his ambitions. By shrouding himself and his organization in a cloak of "respectability," Pendergast would have a much better chance of extending his power into new areas.

Pendergast was entirely too ambitious to rest on his laurels. Even though he had won control of the city government, his victory had been precariously close. Thus he immediately embarked upon a program to broaden his following in Kansas City. Such a program, if successful, would have a dual effect. In the first place, it would ensure his continued domination of the city. And second, the larger the majorities that he could turn out of Kansas City and Jackson County on election day, the more would be enchanced his state-wide prestige and power in the Democratic party.

One of the first things that Pendergast did was to make an effort to extend his organization into all of the city's wards. As we have seen he already had a solid organization in the North Side wards, where the inhabitants were given welfare services by his lieutenants. In neighborhoods that housed the Irish, Italians, Negroes, and other low-income groups, the Pendergast machine functioned after a pattern much like that of the classical political machine described in every historical survey of the Gilded Age. The traditional machine handouts of food, fuel, and clothing, as well as aid in finding employment and help when in trouble with the law, were services that ingratiated the machine with unfortunates of the North Side. However, the majority of Kansas City's population was middle class, and for Pendergast to expand his machine he needed a different kind of organization. For example, in the mid-1920's less than 6 per cent of Kansas City's registered voters were foreign-born. The Negro population was larger than in some major cities, but by 1930 less than 10 per cent of the Kansas City population was colored. Primarily a mercantile and financial center, the metropolis in the heart of America was populated by a large native-American middle class. The local chamber of commerce liked to advertise Kansas City as "the most American city" in the nation.

Pendergast intensified his efforts to expand the organization throughout the entire city, including the many residential wards. One of the ways that he went about this was to build an organization in every ward, primarily through the creation of political clubs in the several wards. Pendergast was wise enough to see that he could not enlist the services of ward and precinct captains in middle-class residential neighborhoods by providing them with the necessities of life such as food and clothing—they already had those things. However, there were other services that could be provided. One such service which drew countless people into the organization was primarily social in nature. Significantly, the political clubs in each ward did not function just at election time. They were active throughout the year. Most of the clubs sponsored weekly or monthly bridge parties and teas for the ladies. Some of the clubs held dinners, dances, picnics, and parties for both men and women. For the young active male members the organization had a baseball league with a team in every ward. And for those who wanted physical activity in the winter, Tom's nephew, Francis, organized a bowling league. In these various ways then, the Pendergast machine provided a social outlet for many citizens who could not afford to belong to the city's expensive and exclusive country clubs. In return, those who reaped the social benefits from the organization's clubs, knocked on doors at election time and urged their neighbors to vote for the Pendergast slate.

The Jackson Democratic Club, which had been organized in 1890 by Alderman Jim as the city's first permanent Democratic organization, became known as the parent club of all of the others. The little hole-in-the-wall office on the North Side had been Pendergast headquarters for years. But in 1926, because the Jackson Democratic Club was to co-ordinate all of the other clubs in the city, Pendergast had it moved to a more central location at 1908 Main Street. The new location was more easily accessible to club members from all over the city, and the second-floor headquarters was larger and could now accommodate the expanding organization. Boss Tom, who gave himself the title Chairman of the Executive Board, had a conveniently arranged office where he could meet with Democrats during his office hours. And across the hall was a large assembly room for organizational meetings, plus some smaller conference rooms.

When the headquarters club was moved to its central location, Jim Aylward became Pendergast's right-hand man. Aylward was placed in charge of organization, and he was largely responsible for building the clubs throughout the city. He soon became invaluable, as chairman of the Jackson County Democratic party, by building up Pendergast support throughout the entire state.

Aylward was aided in his work by a newspaper, the *Missouri Democrat*, which the organization had started publishing in late 1925. The paper was published in Kansas City, and was clearly the organ of the Pendergast machine. The paper never officially announced that it was run by Pendergast, but James T. Bradshaw, a loyal follower who lost his state appointment when Republican

Governor Hyde took office, became the editor. It is significant that the paper began when Pendergast was on the threshold of controlling Kansas City, and folded within a few months after he went to prison. The paper supported only Pendergast candidates at primary election time, and it continually published extremely favorable articles about Pendergast. Every time a controversy arose, either within the party, or in the city, county, or nation, Tom Pendergast's viewpoint was set forth as the only sound solution.[10]

The *Missouri Democrat* became a handy instrument for the machine. Its audience reached beyond Kansas City Democrats, for by the 1930's United States Representative Clarence Cannon, who was no Pendergast partisan, observed that the *Missouri Democrat* "is unquestionably a most effective organ in reaching the local politicians around the county courthouses . . . and in quietly molding editorial opinion in the country press." [11] If this very successful Missouri politician was correct, the paper no doubt aided Aylward in his drive to build up support for Pendergast candidates throughout the state.

The machine organ was obviously important on the local level. Aylward used it to publicize ward club meetings and special events, and he used it to praise various workers in the organization for the work they were doing for the party. This little bit of psychology was surely effective. Photographs or articles on various workers certainly served as an impetus for them to work even harder, and perhaps encouraged others to vie for the little honors as well.

The machine also used the *Missouri Democrat* to win support in the local business community. Occasionally, feature articles were run on selected companies and businessmen. The little paper was only eight pages long so it had to be selective in its coverage. But in an early issue a large feature article was run, complete with photographs, on Fred W. Fleming and Francis M. Wilson, who were the receivers of the Kansas City Railways Company, the firm that Pendergast had helped in its quest for a new franchise in 1914.

The article had unstinted praise for the job that these two businessmen had done in restoring the bankrupt company. The president of Kansas City Life Insurance Company, Joseph B. Reynolds, was likewise honored with a photograph, along with an article praising him for donating $100,000 to William Jewell College. In the same way, the Kansas City Public Service Company was praised because "it knows the needs of the public and meets all requirements of service at the lowest possible rates." [12]

The newspaper was not only used to help build the organization and to gain support for the machine in the business community, it was also used to help build the new image of Tom Pendergast. Photographs were published each year showing Pendergast's Christmas dinners for the poor in the North End, but it was clear that Boss Tom was not down there running them anymore. He was the benefactor, but now he was aloof. His lieutenant Charlie Clark was the man who officiated. The onetime ward boss had not only turned over the direction of the old bailiwick to his ward heelers, but he might well have appeared incongruous if he had gone back there. His newspaper publicized his new home far to the south on exclusive Ward Parkway. The photographs of him in the *Missouri Democrat* were usually with his wife. The smiling couple was dressed in the latest fashion, and often discovered by a photographer just as they were preparing to sail for Europe. Presented as a family man and stylish world traveler, Pendergast liked to bolster the new image by referring to himself as a successful businessman.

The new image made Pendergast more acceptable to those who moved in fashionable circles. By the mid-'thirties he could drop in on a man like Herbert M. Woolf, the owner of Kansas City's most exclusive men's clothing company. The boss was welcome, and he obviously had won the respect of Woolf, and was able to influence his political convictions. For example, Woolf wrote to gubernatorial candidate Lloyd Stark on one occasion that "while I do not know you personally, was talking to T. J. Pendergast yesterday and, from what he tells me, you are the type [of] man that we should have in the Governor's chair, and I will be very glad to help you all I can." [13]

At the same time that Pendergast was moving in higher circles and ingratiating himself with those in the upper walks of life, he did not cut himself off entirely from his old associates. Although he did not go down to the North Side wards and personally tend to his following there, the indigents, unemployed, and party workers from the old neighborhoods were always welcome to come to the Ready-Mixed Cement Company or the Jackson Democratic Club and call on the boss to discuss politics or ask for favors. Pendergast opened one or the other office every day to anyone who cared to call. He would hold personal interviews with everyone who came to the headquarters, and he met them one by one in the order that they arrived. No special consideration was given to any caller, regardless of his wealth or position. Each individual sat down and waited his turn to see the boss—it was a first come first served basis. Lloyd Stark, for example, the wealthy nurseryman and influential rural politician, drove over two hundred miles to see the boss. And he sat down and waited his turn just like everybody else who called on Boss Pendergast. [14]

In many ways, then, Pendergast gradually extended his influence in Kansas City and at the same time maintained his hold on his old following. Perhaps even more important to him in strengthening his organization, though, was the power that was his when his faction took office under the new charter in January 1926. Pendergast's majority on the city council immediately appointed Henry F. McElroy city manager. McElroy had been a Pendergast partisan for years, and had been elected to the county court along with Harry Truman a few years before.

When McElroy took office he remained loyal to the organization that appointed him. He demonstrated his disdain for the nonpartisan intentions of those who had drafted the charter. An admitted partisan, the city manager appointed Democrats to direct the eight city departments. He gave the Goats six of the directorships and

Shannon Rabbits were given two in order to promote harmony within the party. On top of this, there was a monthly payroll that grew to an average of $450,000 for approximately 3700 men. And eventually there were half-time jobs of $24 per week that added nearly $120,000 to the city payroll monthly.[15]

This extensive patronage was an advantage of immeasurable value to the Pendergast machine. With so many jobs to offer as rewards it is no wonder that Jim Aylward could announce by 1932 that he had "close to 12 workers to the Precinct, and as there are 458 Precincts this force constitutes a formidable army of active, energetic Democrats."[16]

Control of the city administration gave Pendergast patronage to help him extend his organization in Kansas City, but it gave other advantages too. It has already been pointed out that through his newspaper Pendergast did his best to win the support of the business community. However, the control of the city government allowed him to provide even more services to local businesses. One extremely significant way that Pendergast was able to broaden his support to include the business community was by offering them tax favors. Some investigators for Governor Stark discovered, for example, that large railroad and utilities companies in Kansas City had received huge tax abatements from the Pendergast-controlled government. The Kansas City Power and Light Company, the Kansas City Terminal Railroad Company, and the Kansas City Public Service Company all had thousands of dollars in taxes returned to them.[17]

There were still other ways that the machine won favor in Kansas City. During the prohibition era, for example, not all of the local citizens appreciated the virtues of the Eighteenth Amendment. Indeed, many wanted to drink liquor, and when the Pendergast machine was in power it was much easier to do. Restaurants, hotels, and "soft drink" bars all over the North End and West Bottoms sold whisky to thirsty customers. Several of the speakeasies were notorious. One, the Centropolis Hotel, was continually under attack by the "drys." John M. Kennedy, judge of the North Side Court, and a member of the Pendergast machine, was once arrested for drinking whisky in the hotel. But the boisterous judge had friends in the right places. Consequently he was not booked.[18]

Columnist John Cameron Swayze, a former Kansas Citian, had some vivid memories of speakeasies. He recalled that

> . . . speakeasies had everything except the swinging door, and a picture etched on memory is that of an alert waiter, attired in stiffly-starched white jacket, sitting primly in the front seat of a police car parked outside of a "speak." He was listening for calls on the police radio as the officers of the law tarried at the bar within.[19]

Even after prohibition ended, the Pendergast machine protected lively night spots for entertainment-seekers in Kansas City. Some of the nation's best jazz was born and nurtured in the bars that remained open long after closing hours. The music of Count Basie and his "Kansas City Seven" could be heard almost any night at the Reno Club on Twelfth Street. Bennie Moten, Paul Banks, Jay McShann, Andy Kirk, and George E. Lee could also be heard nightly in one of the city's fifty or more nightclubs on Twelfth and Eighteenth streets.

An authority on Kansas City jazz wrote that "by the mid-1920's Kansas City was in full swing. It was an incubator, a jazz breadbasket for the Southwest. According to musicians who lived and worked here between 1925 and World War II, it must have been one long twenty-year jam session." [20] A pianist who played in one of the clubs, George Salisbury, fondly remembered it this way: "Why man, there wasn't nothin' like it! Kaycee was going. And when Ah say 'going' Ah mean our cats played around de clock 'n' nobody slowed down. When a man stepped out on Twelfth Street —he was out!" [21]

Exciting music came out of the El Torreon Ballroom, Fairyland Park, and the Sunset and Subway clubs. And the voice of the blues singer, Julia Lee, touched the hearts of many listeners at the

Yellow Front Saloon. There were other entertainment spots too, but they upset the more puritanical citizens. There were the bawdy houses on Thirteenth and Fourteenth streets, and there was the Chesterfield Club where one could eat lunch and watch strippers.[22]

Almost everyone in Kansas City knew that such places were shielded by the Pendergast machine. No doubt many assumed that the machine raked off a percentage of the profits for itself. Certainly this hurt the organization in some quarters and cost it a few votes. However, there were other citizens who enjoyed these forms of entertainment, and there were also many businessmen who appreciated the fact that outsiders swarmed into Kansas City to take advantage of its night life, which was not available in most midwestern towns.

The many services that his machine could perform for Kansas Citians from all walks of life, plus his effort to extend the organization into all parts of the city, make it understandable why Pendergast was able to broaden his base of power. Indeed, his city tickets received large majorities for re-election in 1930, 1934, and 1938. And the votes came from more than just the North Side wards, they came from all over the city.

The Great Depression caused many voters to back the Democratic party in the 1930's, but Pendergast himself was responsible for drawing much of this support to the Democratic tickets in Kansas City. Pendergast's strength in the primaries shows that his support was the result of more than the Great Depression. He took advantage of the opportunities offered to him by the depression, to extend services to many interest groups in his community.

7

State Control and
Pendergast Democracy

In the 1920's Missourians made a habit of electing Republicans. The Democratic party was out of power, and its political machinery was broken down and decaying. Only one man maintained a significant Democratic machine—Thomas J. Pendergast. His organization won in Kansas City and Jackson County throughout the years of Republican domination with only one exception, which came in 1924. His machine did such a remarkable job of delivering large majorities to Democratic candidates that when the depression came and promised a brighter future for the party, those who found themselves interested again in politics were forced to turn to the man with the organization.[1]

The 1930 city election in Kansas City drew attention throughout the state. Boss Pendergast was making his first bid for re-election under the new charter. One St. Louis Democrat pointed out that if Pendergast's boys "win out in the election tomorrow, they will be in a position to exert a great influence on the future of the party in the State."[2] Pendergast's boys did win—and by a landslide. The victorious boss went to New York soon after the election, and he made sure that his newspaper, which circulated among the state's Democrats, carried a front page article on the warm praises that he received from Al Smith and Jimmy Walker while he was there. In addition, the machine staged a big rally out in the little town of Sedalia. Tom Pendergast arrived at the fair grounds with three thousand followers, and made quite an impression upon the Missouri Democracy.[3]

The following fall, the machine produced its most impressive victory, electing its entire ticket by landslide proportions. Harry Truman led the ticket in his race for presiding judge, winning over his Republican opponent by more than 48,000 votes. And Rabbit boss Joe Shannon, now satisfied to let Pendergast lead, was sent to the United States House of Representatives with the blessing and aid of his old rival.

Pendergast was clearly supreme in Kansas City and Jackson County. Soon, however, events beyond his control would conspire to make him the most powerful individual in Missouri. The depression made Democratic domination of the legislature and governorship almost a certainty and this stroke of fate provided Pendergast with some new opportunities. He quickly made the most of them and extended his power throughout the state.

The fact that Pendergast would direct Missouri's Democratic party was forecast by a politician from Springfield. Writing to Francis M. Wilson, who hoped for Pendergast's support for the gubernatorial nomination again in 1932 after an unsuccessful bid for election four years before, Frank McDavid said:

> It would be a very helpful thing, of course, if the Democrats of the State could know that Pendergast is friendly to you. There is a disposition among Democrats outstate to do some honor to the Democracy of Jackson County for its magnificent work in recent campaigns, and it would be an encouraging thing if friends of yours throughout the State could know that in supporting you they are doing a thing which commends itself to the favor of Pendergast and his followers in Kansas City.[4]

This statement undoubtedly did not reflect the attitude of all Missouri Democrats, but it was indicative of that of some at least.

One Missouri Democrat took a rather practical view of the political scene. He wrote that "In all my years of political experience in Missouri I never met Mr. Pendergast . . . and I presume he has his faults, like the rest of us, but I wish St. Louis had an organization like 'his.' " [5] The truth was that St. Louis did not have an organization like his, and neither did any other part of the state. Therefore when the United States Census demonstrated that Missouri's congressional districts should be reapportioned, and the legislators failed to agree upon how it should be done, fate again was good to Pendergast. Because of the situation, every man who wanted to run for Congress in 1932 had to run at large. With a large block of votes from Kansas City and Jackson County absolutely essential under such circumstances, Pendergast had an unusually large say in preparing the Democratic ticket, which was certain to win in November.

Democrats from all over the state converged upon the Jackson Democratic Club in Kansas City, each one hoping to get the support of Boss Pendergast. Lloyd Stark, who was studying the political terrain in hopes of becoming governor, wrote confidently to a friend that "I would hate to be a Congressman at the next election who was forced to run without Pendergast's active support or tacid [sic] approval." [6] Many other Democrats felt the same way. Clarence Cannon asked for Pendergast's support, received it, and consequently returned to Congress.[7] Other hopefuls were less fortunate. Ewing Cockrell sought the boss's support but was disappointed to find that "he would endorse only a few for Congress." [8] Cockrell, who was not one of the lucky few, ran anyway, and lost.

Pendergast did support one candidate in the 1932 primary who failed to win—Charles Howell of Kansas City, who ran for the senatorial nomination against Bennett Clark. Howell lost but it did not upset Pendergast. He realized before the election that he had erred inasmuch as Howell was a man who was exceptionally unpopular in rural areas, and Pendergast was reportedly "sick of Howell" before the election anyway. Pendergast also had made no secret of the fact that the office he was most intent on winning was that of governor.[9]

The Kansas City boss felt so strongly about the governorship that he made no announcement as to whom he would support in the primary until he was certain which candidate would be the strongest. He knew he could deliver the Kansas City and Jackson County vote, but he wanted to back a candidate who had a large following throughout rural Missouri. Politically ambitious Harry Truman looked for rural support in the spring of 1931, in hopes that Pendergast would give him the organization's backing. Truman's campaign was led by an attorney, James E. Ruffin, who opened the headquarters of a Truman-for-Governor Club in Springfield. Ruffin was aided by representatives from fifteen counties. The county judge had an impressive record behind him of building good county roads, and doing it efficiently. He even completed one road project with less money than the public, in a bond election, had authorized him to spend. But the Truman "boom," as some rural Democrats viewed it, fizzled in a short time. It was Francis M. Wilson of Kansas City, whom Pendergast had backed in 1928, who demonstrated the most rural strength and therefore was given the support of the machine.

Wilson did not go unopposed in the Democratic primary. On the contrary, Russell Dearmont actively campaigned against Wilson, and "bossism" was his issue. Pendergast was attacked as a boss, and Wilson was depicted as a puppet. This proved highly ineffective, even in Dearmont's own St. Louis district. The *St. Louis Post-Dispatch* aided Dearmont in his attack on Pendergast. But as one St. Louis attorney viewed it, the name Pendergast was much more of an asset than a liability. He suggested to Wilson that Pendergast support "will mean many more votes to your candidacy than the *Post-Dispatch* will detract. . . ."[10]

Pendergast support did aid Wilson in St. Louis because the Kansas City boss had an effective working agreement with William

Igoe, an influential St. Louis faction leader. Igoe visited Pendergast at Kansas City in January 1932 and soon after his visit it was clear that he was organizing the "trench workers" in St. Louis for Pendergast's nominee.[11]

Francis Wilson won the primary with ease. He could have won easily in November, but less than a month before the general election he died suddenly from a serious stomach disorder. The state committee quickly assembled to nominate a candidate in his place. Pendergast made it known that he favored the selection of Judge Guy B. Park, who lived just a few miles north of Kansas City in the town of Platte City. Lloyd Stark, however, was a top contender with a significant rural following. Stark refused to withdraw for Park, but Pendergast's friends in St. Louis gave their support to Park and assured the success of Pendergast's goal of electing a governor.[12]

Events beyond Pendergast's control had conspired again to aid him. The depression ensured the election of the Democratic gubernatorial nominee, and an untimely death had allowed Pendergast to hand-pick him. Francis Wilson had been indebted to Pendergast, and if elected he would have been expected to grant the big boss a large share of the patronage. On the other hand, Wilson had a large following that he had gained on his own, before Pendergast ever endorsed him. Also, Wilson was a man of strong character with a mind of his own—a man whom Pendergast never would have dominated. One of the most revealing statements of Wilson's relationship with Pendergast is in a letter which Wilson wrote to the editor of the *The Missouri Farmer*, William Hirth. This editor was anti-Pendergast, and he wanted to print an editorial making it clear that if elected, Wilson would not be "bossed" by Pendergast. Wilson asked Hirth not to print it, and in doing so revealed his relationship with the boss:

> Sometime I want Pendergast to meet you. I think just a brief talk with him will convince you that he has been "more sinned against than sinning." He never tried to improperly influence me in all my public life and if he had I would have told him what

you said I would [in the proposed editorial]. . . . Few know that when Pendergast was a boy, living with his parents in St. Joseph, and [my] father was engaged in his bitter battles with the rich and powerful Burnes crowd in his races for Congress, he went about the town with other boys of his age building bonfires, carrying banners and other campaign [materials] to help father in his fierce fights. Pendergast has never forgotten and neither have I. He is several years younger. And so in all the years that my name has been mentioned in connection with a state office from Attorney-General, almost 30 years ago, to the present, Pendergast has been out front for me. Perhaps I am the only man who was ever a candidate for a state office that did not ask him directly, or through another for his support. I never did. I firmly believe that if elected Governor Pendergast would be among the last to do that which would tend to harm my administration. He knows me and so knows my strict views on a number of matter[s] particularly patronage.[13]

Francis Wilson was a personal friend of the boss. And considering Pendergast's refusal to attempt to dissuade Harry Truman from maintaining a clean, efficient county administration, it is difficult to believe that he would have treated Wilson any differently. Thus Wilson's death placed Pendergast in a position where he had more power than he probably would have had otherwise. His new candidate, Judge Park, had not been a contender for the nomination, and had no strong support behind him other than Pendergast's. An unknown in many parts of the state, Park was in a position of unusual indebtedness to Pendergast.

In approximately three weeks' time, the county judge from Platte City was raised from relative obscurity to the governor's mansion. This would have been a difficult situation for even the strongest willed man, and Governor Park was unable to cope with it. He obviously was not a corrupt man who used his position to make a fortune through graft and corruption. On the other hand, either through an inability to see what was happening, or through a refusal to stand his ground, he allowed Boss Pendergast to run the state—at least in many of the areas that could be useful to his organization.

On occasion the governor apparently resented the way people assumed that Pendergast, not he, made all of the decisions on patronage. In rare instances Park would assert himself and point out that he had not accepted Pendergast's suggestion to employ a particular individual. For the most part, however, Pendergast had much influence at the state capitol. Astutely seizing every opportunity to strengthen his power, he used his influence to help many individuals and many groups both in and outside of Kansas City. In this way the boss was able to maintain a stronger hold on districts that he already controlled, and to extend his power into new areas.

One of the major tools that the Kansas City political leader used to maintain and extend his power was patronage. One of Harry Hopkins's investigators in Missouri noted the Pendergast influence when he wrote to Washington that "it is observable that through Park Pendergast gets the state appointments. The state house is lousy with Pendergast men." [14] Such a comment is not surprising because others noticed the preponderance of Pendergast followers and complained that Pendergast had all of the say on patronage, and that even Joe Shannon was ignored on all major appointments.

As was to be expected, Pendergast took good care of the loyal Democrats in Kansas City, but he also repaid the Republicans who had been helpful to him. Pendergast was given control of the Board of Election Commissioners, which was required by law to be half Republican and half Democrat in membership. The Kansas City Democratic organization made sure that Governor Park selected "co-operative" Republicans from Kansas City and Jackson County for that board. These Republicans not only co-operated with the machine, but also placed straight Republican tickets in the field during Kansas City Municipal elections, in order to weaken the Reform or Fusionist tickets, which were backed by Republicans and Democrats who opposed the Pendergast slates.

Kansas City Republicans were well aware of what was going on. One of them wrote to a rural out-state G.O.P. supporter that "our judges and clerks are 'trimmers,' appointed by Committeemen actually selected by the Pendergast and Cas Welch organizations." [15] Another Republican in Kansas City saw the party in two factions. "On one side of the fence," he wrote, "are the elements in the Republican party that supported our fusion group in the city election, and are thoroughly anti-Pendergast. On the other side is a group of those Republicans . . . who joined hands with Pendergast to defeat the Fusion ticket. . . ." [16] Charles Becker and Charles Orr were two influential Republicans behind this working agreement with Pendergast, who saw to it that their supporters were rewarded just the same as the Democrats. [17]

Pendergast made certain that both Democrats and Republicans who aided him in Kansas City and Jackson County were given a share of the spoils. Moreover, he did not fail to do favors for those who lived in rural areas. Both men and women who worked for the Pendergast organization were rewarded by the powers in Kansas City that ran the state house.

With his extraordinary influence at the capitol in Jefferson City, Pendergast was able to do more than provide jobs for people— although that was no small favor in itself during the depression. But more than that, he provided other services as well. It becomes easy to see why Pendergast had so much support in Kansas City, even in the residential wards, when one realizes how he served his community. Obviously his control of the city administration had allowed him to get things done for Kansas Citians. Indeed, Jim Pendergast remembered how a phone call from his Uncle Tom to the city hall would get immediate action for businessmen who were halted in their operations by red tape or an outmoded city ordinance. But with his new power, he could do even more.

He used his influence continually to aid people in various occupations in Kansas City. On one occasion, for example, he assisted local osteopaths when the graduates of Kansas City's Central College of Osteopathy were being discriminated against by the State Examining Board. [18] At another time, a group of thirty-six Kansas City chiropractors signed a petition which read: "PETITION TO HON. T. J. PENDERGAST We, the undersigned . . .

declare our allegiance to your leadership. . . ." This loyalty was the result of Pendergast support for the doctor this group wanted appointed to the State Board of Chiropractic Examiners.[19] Also, there were those small favors for individuals which the boss could perform by merely writing a letter to the governor, as he did when he requested that Park have the son of a prominent physician admitted to the state medical school.[20]

The Park administration helped Pendergast perform other services—some of which were blatantly illegal. For example, investigations carried out by the governor who succeeded Park in office turned up evidence about improper use of state contracts. This evidence convinced Governor Lloyd Stark's investigators that representatives of the North American Savings and Loan Company in Kansas City, in which Jim Pendergast had an interest, would inform firms bidding for a state contract that the firm which purchased blocks of stock from the savings and loan company would be awarded the contract.[21]

Probably the most flagrant violation of the public trust during this period, which allowed Pendergast to serve a large number of individuals including himself, was an insurance swindle. Governor Park appointed R. Emmett O'Malley, at Pendergast's personal request, to the office of State Superintendent of Insurance. Park's kindness allowed the appointee and Pendergast to perpetrate an insurance deal which ultimately sent both of them to prison.

The roots of the scandalous insurance fraud went back to 1929 when 137 insurance companies doing business in Missouri increased their premiums 16% per cent. Joseph B. Thompson, who was superintendent at that time, refused to approve the increase. The companies, however, obtained an injunction which forbade Thompson to interfere, but it also ordered the 16% per cent to be impounded by the State of Missouri until the case could be settled. For the next four years the rate case continued, and no settlement was made.

Throughout the period of litigation the insurance companies were represented by Charles Street, who was an executive in a

Chicago insurance company. Early in 1935 Emmett O'Malley went to St. Louis and called on A. L. McCormack, the president of the Missouri Association of Insurance Agents. O'Malley offered to settle the case in favor of the insurance companies if McCormack could get Street to pay off Tom Pendergast. McCormack contacted Street, and in a few days Pendergast met the two insurance executives in Chicago. After some negotiation they agreed that Pendergast should receive $750,000 for his service, and then O'Malley would see to it that a "satisfactory" compromise was worked out between the insurance companies and the state.[22]

The pay-off to Pendergast, of which he gave part to O'Malley and McCormack, was of course kept secret. But a compromise was soon drawn up publicly with the advice of attorneys. Of the $9 million impounded, the insurance companies received 80 per cent, and only 20 per cent was returned to the policyholders. Governor Park signed the O'Malley compromise, and many citizens, especially policyholders, screamed "fraud." [23]

Pendergast made a sizable sum of money out of the deal, but obviously he was serving many more interests than his own. During the next administration, when Governor Stark decided that O'Malley should be dismissed, it became clear just how many businessmen had appreciated the state superintendent's "compromise." Stark's correspondence files reveal that many individuals desired to see O'Malley removed. However, a prodigious number of letters poured in from Kansas City and other parts of the state, imploring the governor to retain the superintendent. Major S. R. Toucey, a member of the exclusive Kansas City Club, said that he voted for Stark because he thought he would retain O'Malley.[24] And Howard Austin, president of the Kansas City branch of the Prudential Insurance Company of America, endorsed the corrupted employee.[25] Naturally, countless other insurance company executives came to the compromiser's aid. Letters inundated Stark's office from Kansas City branch managers of many big insurance companies, including New England Mutual and Connecticut Mutual.

Governor Park was criticized by many people for signing the compromise, but it is clear that some influential people who were not insurance executives found the settlement to their liking. The highly respected J. C. Nichols, for example, owner of the J. C. Nichols Investment Company and developer of the beautiful Country Club Plaza in Kansas City, congratulated the governor for his "very constructive piece of work" ending "the insurance war. . . ." Nichols wrote further that

> the unsettled condition in insurance for the last dozen years has placed a penalty, so I am credibly informed, on my properties as well as that of others, which is almost unbearable. The small home owners, as well as the owners of high class buildings have, to my certain knowledge, been paying far more than they would be required to pay were their properties in a state where there is no turmoil over insurance rates. The amount of impounded premiums is comparatively negligible compared with the savings that will accrue to these owners.[26]

Thus Nichols was statisfied with the deal, as were others who derived benefits. O'Malley, one Republican charged, provided several lawyers with fees by enlisting them as "Attorneys for the State" in the case. One of them allegedly was Russell Dearmont, who ironically enough had opposed Wilson in the Democratic gubernatorial primary on the grounds that he was a tool of Boss Pendergast's. Dearmont was taken care of, it was argued, so that he would not try to split the party and oppose Pendergast again.[27]

In the final analysis, this insurance scandal helps us understand why Pendergast was so successful as a political leader. In this case we have the perfect example of his technique. He took a cut for himself, but at the same time he provided something for a diverse community of interests. Lawyers, insurance men, at least one well-known real estate developer, and many property owners (according to Nichols), all derived benefits from the deal. Some of the benefits were legitimate and perhaps worthwhile; others were illegal and obviously corrupt. All in all though, the episode demonstrates society's complexity of interests and points up the political possibilities awaiting those who are clever enough to find areas of agreement among many groups.

The Park administration offered Pendergast countless opportunities to do favors for individuals and interest groups, and thereby expand his organization's support. In the following pages other ways that the governor aided Pendergast will be seen as well. But added to this support from the state capitol in the 1930's came an even more significant ally—the national government.

8

The Pendergast Machine
and New Deal Politics

In Edwin O'Connor's popular novel, *The Last Hurrah*, Frank Skeffington's son cited the reason for his father's defeat in the city election. Like many other city bosses who have been toppled in the past few years, the young man argued, Skeffington's defeat could be explained by remembering one name—Roosevelt. The old-time boss was destroyed, he continued, because Roosevelt took

> away his source of power. He made . . . [that] kind of politician . . . an anachronism. . . . All over the country the bosses have been dying for the last twenty years, thanks to Roosevelt. . . . If anybody wanted anything—jobs, favors, cash—he could only go to the boss, the local leader. What Roosevelt did was to take the handouts out of the local hands.[1]

This analysis is an over simplification—at least in Kansas City. It is true that Tom Pendergast was not an old-time boss in the strict sense, because his power came from serving an extremely broad-based and complex constituency. However, his organization did gain a significant amount of strength by performing the activities of the traditional ward boss, and the New Deal did not end such activities—at least not in the short run. The reason for this is clear. The growing welfare state placed the *source* of handouts and jobs in the Federal government, but it did not alter the all-important function of local *distribution* of such services. Indeed, the Pendergast machine (and probably many others) was actually strengthened by the New Deal. If a local machine was fortunate enough to win the favor of the powers in Washington, it could continue to direct its community's welfare services—and the national government would pay the bill.

Perhaps over a longer period of time the welfare state did hurt the boss, but there are no scholarly studies which demonstrate this.[2] As a matter of fact, if one looks at the criticisms directed against the Daly organization in Chicago in the 1960's, they suggest that city machines still direct many of the Federal welfare programs.

The Pendergast machine did not survive long enough to test this hypothesis. The reason for its demise, however, was not the rise of federally sponsored welfare programs. The Pendergast machine collapsed because of internal corruption which had nothing to do with the welfare state.

Tom Pendergast was not a man to miss opportunities to increase his power, and the New Deal provided just such an opportunity. When the chance came for him to help his organization in Kansas City and throughout the entire state, he was able to take advantage of it. The Kansas City boss managed to win the confidence of Franklin Roosevelt's administration and thereby greatly enhanced his organization's ability to provide services.

Some people have assumed that the Pendergast forces at the Democratic National Convention at Chicago in 1932 alienated Franklin Roosevelt by supporting James A. Reed.[3] But the evidence makes it clear that the story of what actually happened was quite different. Tom Pendergast was in fact behind Roosevelt from the beginning. He realized that Reed never had a chance of winning the nomination, and therefore he manipulated the Missouri delegation to placate Reed and at the same time to aid Roosevelt. Consequently, the Roosevelt administration felt indebted to the Kansas City boss and gave him patronage and control of Federal relief in Missouri.

The Pendergast machine's efforts to win favor with the Roosevelt forces began in July 1931. Ike B. Dunlap of Kansas City, a former classmate of Roosevelt's, and a leading politician in Missouri, was soliciting support for Roosevelt's nomination. Dunlap was to become a member of the Missouri delegation to the national convention, and he kept his New York friend well informed about his chances of winning Missouri's thirty-six votes. As early as the summer of 1931, it was obvious that Tom Pendergast was for Roosevelt, although he felt an obligation to Senator Reed. Dunlap wrote Roosevelt that he had just talked with Pendergast, and the Kansas City boss had said: "If Senator Reed decides to enter the Campaign, I would be required to support him. Secondly, and unless something unforeseen occurs, I will be for Governor Roosevelt, whom I greatly admire." [4]

Pendergast not only expressed an early desire to support Roosevelt, but his organization won favor with James Farley, the chairman of the Democratic State Committee of New York. One week after Dunlap wrote to Governor Roosevelt, Jim Farley came to Missouri seeking support for Roosevelt. He was welcomed with open arms by the Kansas City Democratic organization. Indeed, Jim Aylward took charge of the affair and provided a big luncheon in Farley's honor at the Hotel Muehlebach. By inviting many guests, Aylward was able to give Farley an opportunity to get acquainted with some influential Missouri Democrats. Farley undoubtedly appreciated the red-carpet treatment. From then on he became very close to Pendergast. He visited the leader of the Missouri Democracy on several occasions, and when Pendergast was seriously ill in the late 1930's, he flew to Kansas City to see him.

In the early fall of 1931 Pendergast returned from a trip to New York and made his position clear to the Democrats of Missouri. On

the front page of his organization's newspaper, the boss pointed
out that

> Missouri would be for Senator James A. Reed to a man if our
> own distinguished Democrat were to announce his candidacy for
> the Presidential nomination. We would be for him first, last and
> all the time. If he does not enter the contest, it looks as if our
> delegation would be for Governor Roosevelt. That is what I
> gather from my talks with party leaders. Roosevelt appears to be
> the popular choice all over the country. He has great strength
> everywhere, even in Dry States. I feel sure he would carry New
> York and be elected by a handsome majority.[5]

Pendergast clearly believed that Roosevelt was going to be the
winner, and his statement for the press can hardly be construed
as one that was intended to encourage Reed to make the bid for
the nomination. But the old senator had visions of grandeur, and
he was determined to enter the race regardless.

Pendergast was committed to support Reed, but this did not
prevent him from making some shrewd adjustments when the
Democratic state convention met and selected its delegates to the
national convention. Pendergast felt a certain attachment to Reed
because the old man had been close to the family ever since Alderman Jim gave him his start in politics at the turn of the century.
However, Pendergast was not about to commit political suicide for
a man who was exceedingly unpopular even in his own state.

When the state convention met, it was obvious that the Jackson
County organization held the upper hand. One Democrat who was
there reported, "suffice to say that Pendergast was in complete
control of the Convention machinery." [6] The only serious opposition came from the Dearmont faction in St. Louis, which intended
to battle Pendergast's choice for the gubernatorial nomination,
Francis Wilson. Pendergast's men, however, controlled the cre-
dentials committee, and when the St. Louis delegation was ready
to be seated, Dearmont and his supporters were ousted. In their
places were put the boss's St. Louis allies led by Bill Igoe.

It is significant that with the Pendergast organization dominating the convention, the delegates to the national convention were not placed under a unit rule. Generally, Missouri delegations in the past had been governed by it, but this time Pendergast was against it, and the delegation was instructed "simply to use all honorable means to secure Senator Reed's nomination."[7] Thus after one ballot the delegates would be free to switch to Roosevelt.

A few days after the state convention adjourned, Ike Dunlap wrote to Roosevelt that "Pendergast can be relied on."[8] This became abundantly clear to the New York presidential hopeful. Within a few days Pendergast began conferring with him and Farley on the strategy for the Missouri delegation. The Kansas City boss went to Albany in late May, and there was also some subsequent discussion on the telephone between Kansas City and New York.[9] Pendergast had told Reed that he had no chance for the nomination, but the ex-Senator had refused to withdraw. Consequently, Roosevelt apparently suggested the possibility of Reed as a vice presidential choice, but Pendergast confidentially discouraged the idea because of Reed's "age and dominant personality." He did, however, think that he could "handle" Reed on the first ballot, or even before, if the old man could be informed that he would have some recognition such as secretary of state or attorney general.[10]

These suggestions never materialized, but the Missouri delegation gave Reed his little honor on the first ballot. Some delegates actually switched to Roosevelt before the totals were announced. Several others switched on the second ballot, but one who was ready to do so recalled that "there were several other votes in our delegation ready to go to the President but [they] were held back as Mr. Farley told me that he wanted us to give the President a few on every ballot."[11] Perhaps the way things turned out, Farley actually wanted more votes from Missouri each time than he received. But regardless, after Roosevelt's election, Farley told Senator Bennett Clark, (who was criticizing Pendergast for backing Reed), "Oh, Pendergast was all right. Was with us all the time.

Reed had him hog-tied but I saw him every day and he was with us from the start." [12]

The story of Pendergast's role in the nomination of Roosevelt is complex, but several factors are clear. First of all the Missouri boss favored Roosevelt from the outset; second, he allowed the Missouri delegation to be free from the unit rule so that it could gradually switch to Roosevelt, and he attempted to get Reed to back out and support Roosevelt before the convention; and finally, he convinced Farley that his desire was to aid Roosevelt. As a result, Pendergast won the favor of Roosevelt's administration, and he maintained it until the late 1930's.

Soon after Roosevelt took office, Jim Farley explained to Senator Bennett Clark that a share of Missouri's patronage had been promised to Pendergast before the national convention. Likewise, he argued that Roosevelt felt indebted to the Missouri politico.[13] The new President did much to keep his promises and fulfill any obligation that he felt.

At the very outset of the New Deal, Pendergast went to Washington to ask a favor. The boss's friend and long-time associate, Conrad Mann, was in serious trouble. He had been found guilty of involvement in an illegal lottery in Missouri and sentenced to Federal prison. His life had never been completely spotless. Indeed, it should be recalled that Mann had worked side-by-side with Pendergast in the 1914 street railway franchise election, when they helped make a mockery of the democratic election process by purchasing votes and bribing repeaters. But Mann had managed to maintain a clean enough record in subsequent years to become a highly respected president of Kansas City's chamber of commerce and a leading spokesman for the local Republican party. Although he was a member of the G.O.P., Mann always seemed to find merit in the proposals of the local Democratic organization. For example, in early 1929, before the depression, City Manager McElroy outlined a "Ten-Year Plan" for Kansas City and Jackson County. The plan called for bond issues to finance an extensive public works program for the metropolitan area. The Pendergast image of respectability was bolstered when the president of the chamber of commerce publicly endorsed the proposal.

The local citizenry did not seem to be quite as excited about the Ten-Year Plan as Mann was; therefore it took over two years of planning and campaigning before it could be presented to the voters with any chance of success. Thanks to the diligent work of McElroy, Mann, and Harry Truman, the proposal won acceptance in the spring of 1931. After the election, Pendergast's *Missouri Democrat* carried a large photograph of Truman, Mann, and Mc-Elroy, viewing the return from the special election. The newspaper praised the three men for being instrumental in winning support for the bond issue.

Mann not only added his prestige to the organization's Ten-Year Plan, but he defended the boss-controlled city from critics who were beginning to attack it for housing a growing criminal element.[14] Undoubtedly, as president of the chamber of commerce, Mann would have wanted to protect the image of Kansas City regardless of who controlled it. But no matter what his motives were, Tom Pendergast appreciated the help. Therefore when the civic leader was sentenced to prison, Pendergast went to the rescue. His newspaper ran a front-page story on Mann's conviction defending his actions and arguing that the lottery was merely an "enterprise intended to raise a vast sum for emergency relief." [15]

Roosevelt had taken office by the time Mann was to be imprisoned, and the leader of Missouri's Democracy rushed to Washington in hopes of using his influence to get Mann pardoned. Roosevelt refused to see Pendergast on the grounds that he did not personally take up questions regarding presidential pardons. Never one to be easily discouraged, Pendergast left the White House and went directly to his friend Jim Farley in New York. Roosevelt did not handle such things directly but he obviously did not mind their going through Farley—because Mann received his pardon.

Jim Farley's efficiency in handling that affair for his Kansas City friend led Pendergast to call on him shortly thereafter for another favor. Missouri Congressman-at-large Ralph Lozier was faced with a serious political problem. A lawyer who resided in Lozier's rural district, John C. Atterbury, desired a Federal appointment. Inasmuch as Atterbury and his family had done much to help Lozier get elected, the representative felt obligated to secure him a position. However the congressman was having no luck in Washington in finding him a position. Thus Lozier wrote Pendergast, "I know you have great influence with Mr. Farley and your personal endorsement will insure Mr. Atterbury's appointment, if Mr. Farley is given to understand that you are in earnest in urging his appointment." [16] Always striving to be of help, Pendergast contacted Farley. Roosevelt's associate promised to do what he could. In a few weeks Atterbury was manager of Home Owners' Loan Corporation in his district's office at Moberly, Missouri.

There were still other ways that the New Deal aided Pendergast. It appears that Secretary of Labor Frances Perkins arranged the appointment of a Republican, Martin Lewis, as state director of Federal Re-employment for Missouri. The Democrats, however, were unable to see in Lewis the virtues that the Secretary of Labor did. Thus the Republican was ousted with Senator Bennett Clark's help, and Judge Harry Truman was given the job. Truman wanted the Federal position, but he accepted it on the condition that he be allowed to fulfill his term on the county court. The condition was granted and he took over his new duties, but voluntarily refused the $300 per month salary because he remained on the county payroll until his term expired.

The machine's control of Federal Re-employment for Missouri was a help, but the Civil Works Administration became an even more important boon to the organization. City Manager McElroy always maintained that he gave Harry Hopkins the idea for the CWA, which the latter inaugurated in late 1933. The resourceful McElroy had developed a successful city program to put Kansas City's unemployed to work during the first winter of the depression. Labor-saving equipment was put aside whenever possible, and local male citizens were given picks and shovels to dig water mains or prepare the sewage-carrying Brush Creek for a more sanitary bed of Pendergast's Ready-Mixed concrete.[17] Thousands were employed on McElroy's projects, and the city continued the program after the first winter. Whether or not the Kansas City work relief projects alone inspired Hopkins, it is difficult to say. However, by July 1933, and perhaps even earlier, the New Deal relief administrator did have investigators in Kansas City studying McElroy's program. And in October 1933, just before Hopkins suggested the CWA concept to Roosevelt, he conferred with Missouri Re-employment director, Harry Truman, and no doubt learned more about the Kansas City projects.

Regardless of how much influence McElroy's projects had on Harry Hopkins, once the CWA went into operation, the Pendergast machine was given still more jobs to offer the local citizens. The CWA lasted less than a year, but by February 1934, the Pendergast organ reported that 100,000 men and nearly 10,000 women were employed under the CWA in Missouri. Just how much of this patronage was controlled by the Pendergast organization is impossible to say. However, the evidence indicates that Pendergast maintained full control of the Kansas City part of the program.[18]

Much Federal money also came to Kansas City for construction purposes. Added to the city and county funds, this aid helped the machine boast about the face-lifting that it gave the Missouri metropolis. In a "Progress Edition" of the *Missouri Democrat*, significantly published just before the 1938 city election in Kansas City, editorials and photographs demonstrated how much the city administration—and Pendergast's Ready-Mixed Concrete Company—had done to further the progress of Kansas City. The boss's cement went into a new city hall, court house, police station, and municipal auditorium; and the New Deal helped Pendergast make it all possible through the successor to the CWA—the Works Progress Administration.

The WPA enabled the Kansas City boss to beautify Kansas City, but perhaps even more important was his control over all of the WPA jobs. In less than a week after the WPA was established and Hopkins placed in charge, Matthew S. Murray was appointed director of Federal public works in Missouri. When Murray was named to the Federal position in 1935, he was on City Manager McElroy's staff as director of public works for Kansas City. He had held that post since 1926, and prior to that time he had been with the Missouri state highway commission. Murray was a loyal member of the Pendergast machine. A political associate of Tom Pendergast's in Kansas City described him to Lloyd Stark in the following way:

> You know he is an outstate man; is extra close to T. J. [Pendergast], and has proven himself LOYALTY itself to the man. Murray came here thru Willie Ross of the Ross Construction Company [of which Pendergast was part owner], off the State Highway Department. . . . He was unknown to T.J.P. Yet, he played ball, made good and soon was a schooled and close mouthed public official. . . .[19]

Murray's appointment was a tremendous boon to the Pendergast machine. With control over all of the WPA jobs, the organization was able to strengthen its position in Kansas City and throughout the state. However, if Harry Truman had not been elected to the United States Senate in 1934, it is highly doubtful that Pendergast would have been the recipient of this rich plum.

The WPA director for each state was appointed by Harry Hopkins upon the recommendation of each state's two senators. Bennett Clark of St. Louis was the senior senator from Missouri. He had won the senatorial nomination in 1932 over Pendergast's opposition. Although Pendergast supported him in the general election that year, the Senator remained opposed to Pendergast's dominant role in Missouri politics. In the 1934 primary election, Senator Clark supported Jacob L. (Tuck) Milligan in a four-cornered race with John Cochran, Harry Truman, and an unknown named Cleveland. Clark hoped to nominate Milligan so that he would not have to share the spoils with Pendergast. But because Pendergast was powerful enough to have Truman nominated, Clark surrendered after the primary and co-operated with Pendergast. The Senator made peace with him because he was convinced that he would need the boss's support for his own renomination and election in 1938. To win Pendergast's favor, he joined Senator Truman in 1935 in endorsing Murray for the public works directorship.

The story of Truman's victory in 1934, and Clark's consequent surrender to Pendergast, is one of the most fascinating in the annals of Missouri politics. The battle for the senatorial nomination was unusually bitter. Clark took to the stump for his candidate, Tuck Milligan, who came from Richmond, a little town in northern Missouri. The Senator did all that he could to curb Pendergast's power. He charged that Kansas City's municipal employees were being assessed to support Truman's campaign, and that most of the state employees were being forced into line. In much the same vein Milligan attacked Truman by arguing that Governor Park's administration was doing so much for the Kansas City machine's candidate that the executive mansion would be more appropriately named "Uncle Tom's Cabin."

Truman and Cochran put on less flamboyant but much more intriguing campaigns. Some evidence suggests that Tom Pendergast played a shrewd game and brought both Harry Truman and John Cochran into the race against Milligan. Pendergast's hand in Truman's entry is no mystery. The Kansas City boss had offered his support to Joe Shannon, who had declined because of ill health and old age.[20] Jim Aylward was promised the machine's backing but he refused it because he had no interest in running for office. After Aylward refused to enter the race, he and Jim Pendergast called on Harry Truman and asked him to run. He accepted, although his heart had been set on running for county collector.

The precise events that took place after Truman agreed to run for the nomination are not clear; but it appears that Pendergast made one of the shrewdest moves of his political career in his effort to win the senatorial race. A political observer in St. Louis suggested that Pendergast had a trick up his sleeve, writing that "Pendergast never did hunt ducks with a brass band. It has always been hard to tell what he is doing, but easy to tell what he has done the day after the election." [21] The St. Louis politician who wrote this letter, G. H. Foree, wrote a series of letters to E. Y. Mitchell, a leading Democrat, in which he reported on what he was discovering about the senatorial race. This man was a perceptive observer because he quite accurately predicted that Clark would see that he could not defeat Pendergast's powerful organization. He also prophesied that after the 1934 primary, Clark would jump on the Pendergast bandwagon and do what Truman and the boss wanted, in order to obtain the machine's support in 1938.

Foree maintained that if Truman could get the Igoe-Dickmann faction in St. Louis to endorse him he would defeat Milligan. When Congressman John Cochran of St. Louis entered the senatorial race against Milligan and Truman, Foree argued that he was placed there to take votes away from Milligan. He said that a dummy candidate was put in the congressional primary in place of Cochran, and that as soon as the primary was over, that individual would withdraw and Cochran would run and succeed himself for Congress in the general election. This plan was arranged, according to Foree's account, when Joe Shannon went to St. Louis and had a conference with Bill Igoe and John Cochran and later when Igoe went to Kansas City for a second meeting. Cochran himself went to Kansas City and called on Pendergast, and immediately after the series of conferences Cochran entered the senatorial race.[22]

This is not an implausible analysis when several other factors are considered. As was pointed out earlier, Pendergast had been working closely with the Igoe-Dickmann faction in St. Louis. It is significant too that Pendergast supported Cochran in 1932 for the congressional nomination. Cochran was a member of the Igoe group. Indeed, he had been Igoe's secretary when the St. Louis faction leader was a member of the United States House of Representatives. It is interesting as well that the Pendergast press somewhat prematurely announced that if Truman decided to enter the race, he would have the Igoe-Dickmann faction's support, suggesting that an agreement had already been consummated be-

tween the St. Louis men and Pendergast. And even more fascinating is the fact that, just as Foree predicted, Cochran lost in the
primary but ran for re-election to Congress that November, and
won.

It seems safe to assume that there was an agreement between
Pendergast and Igoe. Politics often makes strange bedfellows, but
this relationship is perfectly understandable. Both Pendergast and
Igoe had an interest in seeing Bennett Clark's power curbed.
Therefore it is not at all unnatural that they would work out a
plan together. Igoe's faction could have merely supported Truman
over Milligan but it was much wiser to place another man in the
race who was from St. Louis. In this way Cochran, a well-known
congressman, would have a much greater chance of cutting into
Clark's area of strongest support than would a Kansas City man
who was not as well known in the eastern part of the state.

In any case the Pendergast machine did all that it could for
Truman in the campaign. Robert Holloway, the secretary of the
Missouri Public Service Commission, was granted a leave of absence to take charge of Truman's Jefferson City headquarters.[23]
In some areas of the state Governor Park's state employees were
working for Truman, and some were required to help finance his
campaign. One employee of the state wrote to the governor that
"the Grain Department and Police Department are thoroughly
organized and there are few who have not fallen in line. . . . All
of we heads of departments are strong for and working daily for
Mr. Truman." [24]

Jim Aylward, who was by that time chairman of the Democratic
State Committee, and therefore had connections all over the state,
directed the Truman campaign. Truman, however, had some assets
of his own which surely provided him with additional support. His
excellent record as county judge certainly helped, and no doubt
made it easier for such respected individuals as William T.
Kemper, Jr., the son of a prominent Kansas City banker, to promote a Young People's Truman-for-Senator Club. The candidate's
early life helped too. For example, a rural Missouri newspaper, the

St. Clair County Democrat, gave its editorial support to Truman because he, "unlike the other candidates seeking the office, was born on a farm. He was reared between the plow handles. . . ." [25]

Truman's own assets, plus the well-organized support from the extensive Pendergast machine, enabled him to win by slightly more than 40,000 votes over Cochran, who placed second. Milligan ran a poor third, and Cleveland was barely in the race. Cochran carried the city and county of St. Louis by large majorities and thereby demonstrated the wisdom of the deal between Igoe and Pendergast.

Truman's victory was a great triumph for Pendergast. Bennett Clark had challenged the Kansas City boss, but the morning after the election newspapers all over the state proclaimed "Pendergast as the undisputed boss from one end of the state to the other." [26] Therefore, as Foree had predicted, Clark began thinking of his own political future. As one of Stark's political cohorts observed, "what Bennett wants above all else is renomination in 1938." [27] The price that he had to pay in return for Pendergast's support was summed up a few months later by a friendly attorney: "I am rather fond of Clark," wrote Haywood Scott. "He was quite independent when he first went into office. Now he realizes, of course, that he must go along with Pendergast or be defeated for the nomination." [28]

One of the ways that the senior senator's loss of independence manifested itself was in his willingness to help the Pendergast machine obtain aid from the Roosevelt administration. The New Deal had contributed much to Pendergast's strength but Murray's appointment as director of Missouri's Federal work relief was by far its most important contribution. Clark joined Truman in recommending the Pendergast lieutenant for the job, and Harry Hopkins granted their wish.

It was clear that the machine controlled the relief program. When one woman wrote Governor Park and asked for assistance in getting employment with the WPA, he replied that she must get in touch with Mr. Murray of Kansas City because he "will be in complete charge of Federal work relief in Missouri." [29] Even

Senator Truman refused to help individuals find Federal relief employment without first going through the machine. When one Kansas City man sought the Senator's support, Truman replied that "if you will send us endorsements from the Kansas City Democratic Organization, I shall be glad to do what I can for you." [30]

One close associate of Tom Pendergast's wrote to Lloyd Stark, who was to be Governor Park's successor, that with this big Federal aid program, and "with Murray in the saddle to see that it is administered . . . [you know] just what is to be reckoned with [because] . . . we are not fools." [31] They were not fools, and Stark soon discovered how advantageous the WPA could be to a candidate for office. Indeed, in his campaign for the gubernatorial nomination he received Pendergast's support, and sworn testimony shows that some WPA employees voted for Stark under threat of losing their jobs. [32] Again when Stark ran successfully in the general election in 1936, it is clear that he had some Federal employees working on his behalf. [33]

Through its control of the WPA, the Pendergast machine added to its growing state organization. Federal employees in counties throughout the state worked for Pendergast's candidates. Many of the district directors were awarded their jobs because they were supporters of the Kansas City boss. In return these directors did their utmost to encourage the thousands of WPA employees to vote for the machine's candidates. Some employees were merely asked to vote the Pendergast way, but others reportedly were told that if the boss's ticket did not win, the WPA would be withdrawn from Missouri. This employment lever became so effective that in one state campaign for the Democratic nomination to the state Supreme Court, the anti-Pendergast candidate wrote off all hope of winning in several counties because of the WPA strength that the machine had mobilized. [34]

By using the WPA to its own advantage, the Pendergast machine was able to add an important dimension to its growing state organization. When this is coupled to the other benefits already mentioned that Pendergast derived from the Roosevelt administration, it becomes clear that the New Deal did not destroy the basis for machine politics in Missouri—at least not in the short run. Ultimately, the Roosevelt administration helped destroy the Pendergast machine, but that was not because the New Deal made bossism obsolete. On the contrary, it was because Pendergast made some costly mistakes, and the chief executive decided that it would be to his own political advantage to side with the boss's opponents.

9

The Collapse

By mid-year in 1935, Tom Pendergast appeared invulnerable. His organization controlled the Kansas City and Jackson County administrations. The boss reigned supreme at the state capitol, and the entire Federal work relief program was under his direction. He had built a remarkable machine by trading jobs and services for support at election time. This large, patronage-laden organization explains much of his success, although he had even more assets than that by the mid-'thirties. By then, an astutely created image of respectability surrounded the machine and made it easy for people to support. There was a seamy side too, but it was still fairly well hidden.

During the early years of the depression, Kansas City Democrats saw no need to apologize for the leader of their party. The local citizenry as a whole felt little need for a change because, as A. Theodore Brown summarized it, "neither business anxiety nor unemployment was among . . . [Kansas City's] problems. The Pendergast organization, for better or worse, had steered the city through the depression." [1] The city manager continually called attention to the business-like efficiency with which he directed the city government. He pointed out the operating surplus which the city functioned under during those depression years even though it had put many of the unemployed to work. Actually, as subsequent investigations demonstrated, McElroy was juggling the figures to create the intended image, when in fact there existed a one and one-half-million-dollar deficit.[2] For the time being, however, the machine's bookkeeping satisfied the majority of the citizens.

The city manager was not alone in attempting to glorify the organization's image, because Pendergast worked to create an aura of respectability too. During one of his visits to New York, for example, he talked with reporters and bragged about the efficiency of his city government. "Take Kansas City now," he boasted, "we operate there within our income. That is one of the two cities in the country today that hasn't a deficit."[3] And when he was in Chicago on one occasion he reported that after touring several American cities he discovered that Kansas City had less gambling and racketeering than any city its size. "Ours," Pendergast commented, "is a fine, clean and well-ordered town. . . ."[4]

The boss's own activities promoted this appeal to respectability as well. Pendergast regarded himself as a businessman and civic leader. He never tried to hide his success in selling concrete to the city. On the contrary, he argued that he was in a legitimate business, and won the contracts because he sold a good product at the lowest price. The businessman-boss played the role of the civic leader well too. He started an Easter Seal drive in Missouri; and he led a campaign to raise the necessary funds to purchase for the Kansas City-Western Dental College what was "said to be the most complete collection of dental surgical models in the United States."[5]

By 1936 Pendergast had much more support than opposition. No one realized this more than did Lloyd C. Stark. It is ironic that Stark recognized Pendergast's power, utilized it to become governor, and then turned all of the powers of that office upon his political benefactor. Pendergast could not have ruled forever, but there is no doubt that his support of Stark for governor in 1936 hastened the demise of his organization.

Stark was a shrewd politician who wanted very much to be governor—and from there he hoped to go to the United States Senate. The first step in that direction was to win Pendergast's endorsement for the Democratic gubernatorial nomination in 1936. In Missouri a governor was restricted to one four-year term so that Pendergast had to find someone to succeed Guy Park. The Kansas City leader had told Stark that he would promise his support to no one until late 1935. Indeed, the boss wanted to give all interested individuals an opportunity to build a following in rural districts. And then, just as he had done in 1932, he would throw his organization behind the candidate who demonstrated the most rural backing. Stark summed up the boss's position to a friend: Pendergast, he said, was "going to pick the strongest man—the man he thinks is the surest to win." [6]

Stark certainly appreciated the comment of a Kansas City politician's wife who wrote to Mrs. Stark that "we must all bow to the throne which decides affairs of state in the matter of candidates. . . . " [7] The gubernatorial hopeful realized this because he was already sure that whoever won the Kansas City organization's support would automatically get the backing of the St. Louis factions. [8] He made a concentrated effort to win Pendergast's confidence and to build up an impressive show of strength in rural Missouri. Stark was one of the owners of the Stark Brothers Nurseries and Orchards Company, and his correspondence shows that he sent apples to politicians all over the state. He also gained the confidence of Senator Harry Truman, and enlisted his aid. The Missouri Senator promised Stark that he would do all he could for him, and to demonstrate his sincerity he mailed him a list of names of the key men in each county who had worked for him in 1934.

The nurseryman had won Truman's favor, but he was less successful with Jim Aylward. It appears that Aylward did not trust Stark; "Well, if he should be the choice I hope he lives up to the confidences of his many friends." [9] Stark seemed to sense that some influential men in the organization distrusted him because he was continually imploring members of the machine to tell Pendergast that "he need have no fear as regards my loyalty to him and the Organization," and that "I will be just as appreciative after the race as before the race. . . ." [10]

Stark evidently convinced the boss of Missouri's Democratic party that he would be loyal, and that he had the most rural strength. In late September 1935 he mailed to Pendergast a list of names of men and women throughout the state. These people, he informed Pendergast, could be consulted as to the extent of his grass roots support in rural Missouri. Stark then wrote to those people and informed them that "I may send your name in to T. J. P., Kansas City, as one of my outstate political friends. If he should call you in for a conference, he will want to know how strong Stark is in your section. I think you know what to tell him. Just give him the facts, and they are certainly strong enough." [11] Then, after a few phone calls to Pendergast in late September and early October, he received the coveted endorsement.

The organization was at the peak of its efficiency and Stark won the nomination easily. He was elected in November. Former Attorney General Jesse Barrett, Stark's Republican opponent in the general election, had centered his whole campaign on the boss issue—arguing that Pendergast was a corrupt vote stealer, and that Stark would be forced to do whatever the boss asked. However, there appeared to be no great desire on the part of the electorate in 1936 to "turn the rascals out." Indeed, some political observers told Barrett after the election that his campaign strategy had actually backfired. It appears that even some Republicans grew weary of the attacks on Pendergast, who they felt sure was not as bad as depicted by Barrett.

Ironically, however, the Federal district attorney in Kansas City, Maurice M. Milligan, conducted an extensive investigation of the 1936 general election. The evidence which he was to make public about five weeks after the election demonstrated beyond a doubt that the machine was in fact nearly as bad as Jesse Barrett had argued. Election fraud cases were to drag through the courts for the next two years, and disapproval of the machine began to grow. This served as the impetus for the governor to break with Pendergast, and soon the Roosevelt administration followed Stark. It was the beginning of the end for Boss Pendergast.

The question immediately arises as to why the 1936 election scandals were so detrimental to Pendergast. After all, it was by no means the first time that an illegal vote was cast by the organization. It should be recalled that soon after Tom Pendergast took charge of the Goat machine, illegal voting practices began to mar the clean voting record of Alderman Jim's organization. In 1910 Governor Hadley's election commissioners struck many names from the registration lists in the West Bottoms and North End. Similarly, in the special election for the Metropolitan Street Railway Company franchise in 1914, padded registration lists and repeating were commonplace. Again in 1920 the same practices were used, and charges of illegal voting practices came in several subsequent elections.

In the municipal election of 1934, four persons were killed by gangsters who were a part of the Italian arm of the organization. In addition, carloads of toughs drove around the city in black sedans without license plates. They handled roughly some of the workers for the nonpartisan citizens' organization which was attempting to defeat the Pendergast ticket; and the police, whom the home rule law had placed under the control of the city nearly two years previously, ignored the deplorable activities.[12] Governor Park was swamped with telegrams and letters, urging him to use the state police to bring law and order to Kansas City inasmuch as the local force refused to interfere. But, loyal to the boss, he refused.[13]

The rough-house tactics in the 1934 municipal election caused a brief stir, but this was still apparently not enough to shake the people's confidence in the Pendergast machine. In the next city election in 1938, the machine candidates won easily. This is doubly significant because the election was the most honest in years. Gov-

ernor Stark had appointed a new election board without Pendergast's approval. A new permanent registration law was used for
the first time, and there was careful observation at all of the polls.[14]

Perhaps many local citizens were satisfied that Pendergast had
nothing to do with the killings on election day, especially when
some gangsters tried to shoot Henry F. McElroy a week later. They
missed, but came close to hitting his pretty daughter Mary.[15] The
city manager then started a campaign which promised better law
enforcement, and this no doubt appeased some citizens. The city
had had complete control of the police department since 1932, and
so McElroy was able to discharge Eugene C. Reppert, the director
of the department, and replace him with Otto P. Higgins. Added
to this, the Pendergast paper began advertising the low crime rate
of Kansas City. A front page editorial, for example, reported that
the Department of Justice had just released statistics which
demonstrated, the election day murders notwithstanding, that
Kansas City still maintained the lowest crime rate of any city in
its class.

The majority of the people in Kansas City who bothered to vote
apparently were satisfied with the way that the machine covered
up the deplorable events of 1934. But try as they might the leaders
of the Pendergast organization could not cover up the scandals
that followed the 1936 election. The story of the vote fraud cases
appeared in newspaper headlines for the next two years, at the
end of which 259 out of a total of 278 defendants had been convicted. Those who were convicted seemed by and large to be
ordinary citizens. They were not underworld characters like the
gunmen in 1934, rather they were men and women with no previous police records. Even more bewildering was the fact that the
votes which had been stolen in Kansas City in 1936 were not even
needed by the machine for victory. Why, then, were they stolen?
Arthur Krock of the *New York Times* aptly pointed out that

> Any observer of city politics knows the real answer. Each party
> worker of the professional type is an office seeker. From him re-

sults are demanded in exchange for jobs. The better showing he
makes, the higher his standing over rival precinct, ward or district
workers. This competition has led "the boys" to be what the boss
calls "overzealous." [16]

Most voters managed to overlook the election scandals and they
re-elected the Pendergast ticket in 1938. Perhaps because the machine was steering Kansas City through the Great Depression so
effectively, the residents of that city were willing to put up with a
few scandals. But Governor Lloyd Stark did not ignore the sensational, headline-making vote fraud cases, and neither did an increasing number of Democrats in rural districts. The governor's
voluminous correspondence files reveal a growing discontent with
Pendergast's leadership. From the summer of 1937 onwards, letters
began to come congratulating Stark for appointing a board of
election commissioners unsatisfactory to Pendergast. The governor
also was urged to continue his bold, independent action, and to
stop the wide-open gambling in Kansas City.

No doubt when Stark entered the gubernatorial race with Pendergast's support, he did not intend to break his promise of loyalty,
but he thought that his political future might now be enhanced by
an all-out war on the Kansas City boss, whereas before it had been
enhanced by Pendergast's support. After all, the governor could
not succeed himself in 1940. The next best step was to aim for the
United States Senate. Harry Truman would be running for renomination that year, and what could be more advantageous to Stark
than to oppose the Pendergast senator after destroying the corrupt
machine?

More Democrats than Stark had thought of the possibility. Mrs.
Elsie Belle McDaniel, for example, one of the governor's close
political associates, wrote

> Now, Lloyd—please set your sails for U. S. Senator RIGHT NOW—
> and keep on "sawing wood." This thing [the machine] has got
> to break, and you are the ONE person to break it. . . . We are
> *the black spot* in the *whole United States,* and there seems to be

a silent understanding on the part of the majority of our Democratic women, as to our goal.[17]

Stark did set his sails for the Senate, and he began by drawing attention to himself through a series of anti-Pendergast moves. First of all Stark cut down Kansas City's share of state patronage, and this led Pendergast to call him an "ingrate" publicly.[18] But this was only the beginning. Within a few months many state employees who had been recommended by the Kansas City Democratic organization were dropped from the payroll.[19]

The militant Stark moved in other directions as well. He was quite aware of the fact that illegal liquor sales and gambling were going on in Kansas City under the protection of Pendergast's home rule police force. Thus Stark's attorney general, Roy McKittrick, made a serious effort to enforce the laws governing those activities.

Stark did more than merely go over the heads of the Kansas City police to enforce the law. He used all of his power as governor to get the state legislature to return the Kansas City police department to state control. This task he accomplished by July 1939, and when the transition was made corruption was uncovered. Numerous police officers feared losing their jobs once it appeared that the bill ending home rule was going to pass. None of the officers denied the corruption within the department; rather, a rationalization was developed for its existence. One Kansas City lawyer wrote to the governor that "the great majority of our policemen are chivalrous, patriotic men who would rather enforce the law than violate it. They have been acting under orders and would welcome a clean, capable direction. They are disorganized and disturbed with the belief that they are all going to be kicked out." [20]

The new police department reported that almost 50 per cent of the force had to be dismissed. The new chief of police discovered that corruption was general. Offenders who were arrested and taken to district stations were often released by higher-ups. Gambling and other forms of vice were being protected, and criminals from other cities had been finding refuge in Kansas City.[21]

Most of the underworld activities that had flourished under the home rule police had their roots in the Italian sections of Kansas City's North Side. The neighborhood known as "Little Italy" had been part of the larger Pendergast bailiwick since the turn of the century when "King Joe" Damico delivered votes for Alderman Jim on election day. After the elder Pendergast died, his brother continued to run the district. Then, when Tom Pendergast moved out of his old neighborhood as his organization expanded, he left his business partner and political associate, Mike Ross, in charge of the Italian district. Ross held control there until he moved out of the neighborhood himself, and attempted to lead it as an absentee leader. Then, a young Italian named John Lazia, who resented having an Irishman organizing the sons of Italy, built up his own following and in 1928 contested Ross's domination of Little Italy.[22]

Lazia was a handsome young man of slight build. He chewed gum constantly, was extremely articulate, and owned one of the most stylish wardrobes in town. Just before World War I, when he was only eighteen years old, he was sentenced to fifteen years in prison for armed robbery. It was apparent at that time that he was involved with gangland figures because several bold attempts were made to free him. His political connections were also better than average since a Democratic lieutenant governor, substituting for the governor, pardoned him before he had served even one full year.

Lazia's background, added to the way he deposed Mike Ross, foreshadowed what was to come from the Italian North Side in the years ahead. On a special bond election day in May 1928, the ambitious ex-convict literally overpowered Ross and his ward heelers. Lazia's followers roamed the Italian precincts in curtained sedans, kidnapping Anthony Bivona, Frank Benanti, Joe Galluci, and several of Ross's other lieutenants. Within a week after the election Ross had resigned his claims to North Side control, and his ward heelers pledged allegiance to the new leader.

Tom Pendergast was not at all happy about the fall of his ward boss, but Lazia was adamant. Pendergast was always a realist. He needed those North Side votes—from then on he co-operated with Lazia. In return for Lazia's support at election time, Pendergast did favors for him. When the Kansas City boss won control of the police force, the North End leader was given a large voice in local law enforcement. It became common knowledge that the chief of the North Side Democratic Club had friends in the department, and that his illegal gambling and liquor interests operated unmolested.

On top of this, several of the nation's most notorious gangsters managed to get into Kansas City, stay until the pressure abated in other cities, and then leave without police interference. Federal investigators discovered that such well-known criminals as bank robber and killer Frank Nash and his companion Harvey Bailey were playing golf and living well in Kansas City.

The Kansas City police under Pendergast did not capture Frank Nash, but a year later the law enforcement agents in Hot Springs, Arkansas, were more successful. Keeping up its record of hospitality to criminals, Kansas City became the staging area for a sensational plan to free Nash when he was transferred from train to automobile en route to federal prison at Leavenworth, Kansas. Three of the F.B.I.'s most wanted killers, Pretty Boy Floyd, Verne Miller, and Adam Richetti entered the city station on June 17, 1933, and attempted to free their associate. The law men refused to give up their captive without a battle. Thus in what became known as the "Union Station massacre," the gangsters killed four officers and by accident fatally shot Frank Nash too. Leaving five men dead and two others wounded, the killers drove off and spent an uneventful night in the city. They were ignored by police, and Pretty Boy Floyd was given medical attention for the wounds he had received during the gun battle. The next day, Lazia arranged for the three men to be guided safely out of town.

A little more than a year later, the North Side Democratic boss met his own death in a style befitting the activities he protected.

On a summer night in July 1934, he stepped from his chauffeur-driven bullet-proof car and was riddled by machine gun fire and blasts from a shotgun.

Lazia's murderers were never found, and for a while there was tension in the North Side. The police suspected that a rival, Joe Lusco, might have been responsible, but no evidence was ever found to prove that was the case. Before long the situation returned to normal, and the North Side gangsters and politicians accepted the leadership of Lazia's intimate friend, Charles Carollo. The new boss of gangland carried on the tradition of supporting Pendergast, and in return the gambling rackets continued to have police protection.

Federal investigators later discovered that Carollo collected a percentage of the profits from gambling establishments throughout the city. The ex-Lazia lieutenant was found to have given regularly a percentage to Tom Pendergast, and several other members of a local syndicate.

Such conditions caused many local citizens to encourage Governor Stark to end home rule so that Pendergast would lose control of the police department. But there was still an influential portion of the community behind the home rule law-enforcement agency despite the gangland killings and the growing evidence of organized gambling. Business executives, for example, representing twenty-nine Kansas City firms, wrote to a state legislator who was contemplating his vote on the bill to place the Kansas City police under state control. In letters that were all similar in style and content, such companies as Borden's Dairy, Aine's Dairy, Downtown Buick, Berlau Paper Company, and Panama Carbon Company urged this legislator to vote for retaining home rule. The businessmen argued that the police force was much better under home rule than it had been during the days of state control, and that as a consequence their automobile theft and burglary insurance rates had been reduced.[23] Undoubtedly the letters were part of an organized drive to preserve home rule. Although any company would welcome a reduction in the particular insurance rates that were mentioned, it is difficult to believe so many businessmen would be concerned enough about such a minor aspect of their company's overhead that they would feel compelled to write a letter to a state representative without encouragement.

This sizable and obviously well-organized support for the machine's police department demonstrates that in the face of increased opposition to the boss, and despite the growing evidence of vote fraud that had been making headlines for months, the organization still had important local support. The governor's correspondence shows that opposition was increasing, but he remembered years later that once he decided to destroy the machine he had to make a concerted effort to get the majority of the state's Democrats "riled up."

Once Stark had made up his mind to crush Pendergast, he used every weapon in his power to arouse public indignation. The governor was evidently convinced that a thorough investigation of Pendergast's sources of income would produce some startling facts. Thus he called upon the United States Treasury Department to aid him in his fight. The chief of the intelligence unit of that department, Elmer L. Irey, wrote that "it was Stark who asked us to put Pendergast in jail." [24] Stark went to Washington with Maurice Milligan, the Federal district attorney who was heading the Kansas City vote fraud investigations. At their request, some T-Men started an investigation which began by probing into the O'Malley insurance compromise which had been consummated under Governor Park.

While the investigation was being conducted quietly behind the scenes, Stark engaged Pendergast in a primary election contest in 1938. The campaign served the governor's purposes perfectly. In a state-wide race for the Democratic nomination to the state Supreme Court, he could focus public attention upon himself as a reformer who was attempting to reform the state. Likewise, the election would present him with an opportunity to show that he could produce more votes than Pendergast—and thus challenge the boss's right to be recognized as the leader of the party.

Pendergast made it known that his machine would endorse Judge James V. Billings from southeast Missouri. The governor then put a machine of his own into operation behind the incumbent, Judge James M. Douglas. It was a fierce contest because both sides realized that the stakes were high. Not only was the control of the Supreme Court at stake, but more important the entire state as well as the party leaders in Washington waited to see if anyone could successfully challenge Tom Pendergast.

Stark campaigned as a righteous public servant working for the people. He openly admitted that two years before he had sought Pendergast's support just as hundreds of other Democrats had done. But he maintained that when he had asked for Pendergast's support he had no idea that he was expected to connive at corrupt elections and uphold the scandalous insurance agreement. He maintained that he was going to be "Governor of all the People"— not a tool of one man.[25]

The tactics he used to win the nomination for his candidate make one wonder if democracy would ultimately have been any more secure under his leadership of the party than under Boss Tom's. It should be recalled at this point that Stark had nearly complete control of the state machinery since he had not given Pendergast much patronage and had also dropped some of Pendergast's supporters from the state payroll. This gave Stark an advantage in the state-wide race, and he made the most of it. Some state employees were given leaves of absence to campaign for Douglas, and others worked for him on the state's time. Many were forced to contribute 5 per cent of their annual salary to the campaign. All heads of departments were required to display Douglas stickers on their bumpers, and state employees were told to use their own vehicles to haul voters to the polls. On top of this, Stark ordered that two Douglas supporters be in every voting precinct on election day, and that state employees were to handle the task.[26] The pressure became so intense that one of Stark's supporters wrote to him:

if Judge Douglas is not nominated, it will be due in no small measure to the fact that so many Douglas supporters are Douglas supporters under duress, and are Douglas supporters with their fingers crossed. Their friends understand this and govern themselves accordingly.[27]

In earlier years, the Pendergast machine had the most influence in rural areas because when Guy Park was governor the machine had controlled the state machinery. Now, however, Stark was turning the boss's weapons against him. But Pendergast still had one lever to use—the WPA. He had lost the state patronage, but he had WPA workers throughout the state to add to the votes that he already controlled in Kansas City and Jackson County.

Pendergast's control of the WPA worried Stark. Douglas's campaign managers kept him well informed about the strength that Billings was gaining due to the WPA. Federal patronage was so important that the Douglas workers conceded several counties to Billings weeks before the primary. It is no wonder that those on Federal work relief fell into line behind Pendergast's candidate, because some effective tactics were used. Some workers were furnished free drinks by their foremen, and then given a pep talk on the virtues of Judge Billings. No doubt even more effective was the information passed to workers from directors and foremen that the WPA's very existence depended upon Senator Truman, and that if Pendergast's ticket lost, the WPA would be discontinued in Missouri.[28]

Almost a month before the election Stark wired Harry Hopkins, complaining that "Matt Murray, WPA Director for Mo., a leading Pendergast lieutenant, is at Pendergast's direction, using WPA relief rolls in an attempt to defeat Judge James M. Douglas. . . ."[29] Stark received little satisfaction, because a week later he was wiring President Roosevelt: "I am very much disturbed that I have heard nothing from Hopkins."[30]

The governor's concern was not entirely unfounded because even though he had control of the state machinery, Pendergast gave him competition throughout the state. The WPA gave Pendergast some strong rural support, but it still was not enough to overcome the state machine and the growing opposition to the Kansas City organization. Judge Douglas won, and it was a costly loss for Pendergast.

The loss was devastating to Pendergast because it gave President Roosevelt pause and started his asking some questions about Missouri politics. No longer could one automatically equate the Missouri Democracy with the name Pendergast, because Stark was now becoming more and more powerful by attacking him. Roosevelt began to develop a strong attachment to Governor Stark. The President started consulting him on some of the Federal appointments usually reserved as senatorial patronage. One man, for example, was recommended by Senator Truman to be a Federal marshal. Roosevelt refused to accept the recommendation until he consulted with Stark. Farley protested because he felt that this was a Federal appointment and therefore Stark should not be consulted. The President remained adamant because he felt that the Missouri governor might defeat Pendergast in the power struggle.[31]

The fact that Stark was successfully challenging Pendergast and taking advantage of the increasing opposition to the machine's corruption, no doubt encouraged Roosevelt to snub the Kansas City politician. But actually the President had begun deserting his old supporter once the extent of the wholesale vote frauds became evident late in 1936. Federal District Attorney Milligan, who prosecuted the Kansas City election workers, was up for reappointment early in 1938. Senator Truman tried to replace Milligan, who had brought the F.B.I. into the investigations and had gone to Washington with Stark to get the Treasury Department to investigate the boss. But the President, according to Farley, was "cold toward any change in that office."[32]

President Roosevelt's disenchantment with Pendergast led to Maurice Milligan's reappointment. The district attorney had a burning hatred for Pendergast, stemming partly from the boss's refusal to support his brother, Jacob L. Milligan, in his bid for the

Democratic senatorial nomination in 1934. He joined Stark and
F.B.I. and Treasury agents, and labored relentlessly to expose the
corruption that he and many others believed was long-standing.

There was agitation for reform in other quarters too. For several
years Kansas City Rabbi Samuel S. Mayerberg had been attempting to arouse citizens in an effort to overthrow the machine. Dr.
Mayerberg was slight physically, but in terms of intellectual capacity and devotion to civic improvements, he was a giant. He
began his drive for reform in the early 1930's when he was about
forty years old. The Kansas City Ministerial Alliance was one of
the first organizations that he called upon for help. Soon, however,
he branched out and undertook speaking engagements all over the
city, especially before women's clubs. By doing so he managed to
shake a few more citizens out of their apathy. In 1932 someone
tried to kill the crusader. Whether it was a demented anti-Semite
or a gunman hired by the machine, no one knows. In any case, the
courageous Rabbi did not alter his convictions and he continued his
attacks on bossism and organized vice and crime.

The *Kansas City Star* faithfully reported Mayerberg's speeches
and joined his crusade. In the final analysis though, he reached
few individuals except the leaders of the 104 Protestant churches
in the Ministerial Alliance, and a number of activists in women's
club circles. Perhaps Mayerberg was too idealistic to be very effective. On the other hand, it should be kept in mind that he
began his crusade early, when most of the graft and corruption
was still well hidden.

It was clear that Mayerberg's reform movement had made no
headway at all when the returns were counted after the 1938 city
election. The Democratic organization, despite the disclosures of
vote fraud in 1936, won one of its biggest victories. Governor Stark,
Maurice Milligan, and the Federal investigators, on the other hand,
soon met with more success because they did not rely solely on
idealistic appeals to the electorate. On the contrary, they worked
quietly behind the scenes to find evidence that would arouse the
public.

The determination of Stark and Milligan eventually brought five Federal agencies to Kansas City on special assignment. The result was every bit as sensational as they could possibly have hoped. The investigations started with the O'Malley insurance compromise. It was discovered that Pendergast had received $750,000 from the deal, on which he had not paid any income tax. He and O'Malley were charged with contempt on the insurance settlement. A second indictment was brought against Pendergast because an investigation disclosed that he had been guilty of additional income tax evasion from 1927 to 1937. On May 22, 1939, District Attorney Milligan presented the evidence to the court. Pendergast decided to plead guilty to two counts of income tax evasion because the evidence against him was overwhelming. Not only had he made undeclared earnings from the insurance scandal, but over the preceding eleven years he had failed to declare over one million dollars of his income. He had falsified the books of eight different companies in which he held an interest.[33]

Pendergast was sentenced to fifteen months in Federal prison and fined $10,000 on the first count. On the second count the judge set the sentence at three years in prison, but he let Pendergast off with five years of probation. No doubt the fact that the boss entered a plea of guilty partly accounted for the leniency of the court on the second count, but it was certainly taken into consideration as well that he was a very sick man. As a matter of fact, since the summer of 1936, Pendergast had suffered a severe heart attack and had undergone three abdominal operations.

Tom Pendergast spent fifteen months in prison, and several other key men in the machine served time with him. Emmett O'Malley received a sentence for income tax evasion, and so did WPA chief Matt Murray. The director of the police department, Otto Higgins, went to prison for the same offense, and Charley Carollo, a leader in the gambling syndicate, drew an eight-year sentence for using the mails to defraud and failing to pay taxes on his illegal income.[34]

City Manager Henry F. McElroy resigned his office at the city hall immediately after Pendergast was indicted. He died within a few months—before the investigations of his fiscal policies were concluded. It was impossible to discover everything, but what was found was incredible. It was apparent that McElroy had maintained a unique system of bookkeeping. What he had proudly proclaimed was an efficiently conducted city government was in reality a sham which covered an enormous theft of the taxpayers' money. There was a deficit in claims and accounts amounting to almost twenty million dollars. Nearly eleven million dollars' worth of water works bonds had been unlawfully diverted to other uses, and still other bond funds had been used to meet payrolls. Hundreds of thousands of dollars had been lost to the city in tax abatements, and nearly three thousand people were on the city payroll who did nothing but pick up their checks.[35]

Throughout 1939 the newspapers carried stories about new evidence which was discovered almost every day. Much more graft and corruption were discovered, and as a result more members of the machine were sent to prison. With new cases constantly arising which made the vote frauds of 1936 look like petty crimes, it is no wonder that the Citizens' Reform ticket won easily in Kansas City in 1940. The Pendergast machine had won overwhelmingly in 1938, but this time its decimated ranks won only enough votes to carry five of the city's sixteen wards.

Pendergast returned from prison several months after the 1940 city election. He did not live out the five-year term of his probation, for he died in January 1945. Throughout his remaining days he hoped for a presidential pardon and the restoration of his American citizenship. But the pardon never came. Thus his political life ended with his conviction in court on that spring day in 1939.

The blow that ended Tom Pendergast's political career also destroyed his organization. The machine's defeat in Kansas City in 1940 was only the first indication of the devastation that had befallen the Missouri Democracy. In the first general election after the boss went to prison, the normally huge Democratic majorities from Kansas City and Jackson County dwindled to less than half of the usual size. Similarly, the work Pendergast had done to build up a rural organization was little more than a memory because the party collapsed all over the state. Consequently, a Republican governor won in 1940, and three G.O.P. candidates were elected to the United States House of Representatives.

One of the few bright spots for the Democratic party was Harry Truman's re-election to the United States Senate, but his margin of victory was precariously close. Despite his association with the Pendergast machine, Truman had a spotless record. A Federal grand jury and the F.B.I. examined the records of his county court administration, but not a dime was found to have been mis-used and not a penny had been left unaccounted for.[36] It is signifi-cant too that Truman managed to win renomination in 1940, because his two opponents were the men most responsible for bring-ing the collapse of the machine—Lloyd Stark and Maurice Milli-gan. The fact that Truman won attests to his popularity, but it should be pointed out as well that Stark's attack on the machine backfired on his political ambitions. Many Missouri Democrats were disgusted with the growing evidence of corruption under Pendergast's control of the party, but a talk with party leaders who are still alive makes it clear that few men respected Stark for turning against Pendergast.

The general election in 1942 demonstrated that the Republican successes in 1940 were not just temporary. Kansas City and rural Jackson County Democratic votes grew even smaller, and through-out the state the over-all collapse was much more complete. The Democratic candidate for Congress from Missouri's Fifth District in Kansas City and Jackson County won by only slightly more than one thousand votes. He was fortunate though, because he was one of the few Democrats to win in the congressional races. There were thirteen seats available and the Democrats won only four of them.

What had once been a powerful organization was now a sham-bles. Bryce Smith, who had been the Democratic mayor of Kansas City when Pendergast went to prison, summed up the problem faced by Tom Pendergast's nephew, James, when he tried to pull the machine back together:

> Jimmy is trying to whip the organization together again, but I am afraid they are going to have a hard road to travel if they don't keep some of the "old timers" in the background. The *Star* has made the people (and that means a world of votes) believe that whenever any of these old names are mentioned it means crime of the worst sort. Of course this is not the truth, but it is the way the people have been led to think and believe.[37]

It was impossible, of course, to keep the "old timers" in the background. Almost every worker for the Democratic party in Kansas City, and many of those outside the city, had been aligned with the Pendergast organization. Thus the Democratic party itself bore the stigma attached to the Kansas City boss. Jim Pendergast was not able to overcome the obstacles. The Pendergast machine was never revived, and no other organization of any significance has arisen to take its place.

Two years after Pendergast was sentenced to prison, Senator Harry Truman expressed concern over the dwindling strength of his party. He wrote then that "the Democratic Party needs a shot of 'high life.'"[38]   After the Republican victories in 1942, his concern changed to pessimism. "I am very much worried about the Democratic Party in Missouri," he wrote, "in fact it looks as if the future does not hold very much for us right now."[39]

The future did not hold as much success for the Missouri Democracy as the Pendergast era had afforded. The factionalism of the pre-Pendergast period returned and has remained dominant. No leader has been able to construct the necessary machinery to put the party in a position of strength that even approached the heights of power realized for a brief period under the Pendergast dynasty.

Notes

PREFACE

1. "The Study of Corruption," *Political Science Quarterly*, LXXII (December 1957), pp. 502–14.
2. Pendergast is quoted in Jerome Beatty, "A Political Boss Talks About His Job," *American Magazine*, CXV (February 1933), p. 113.

CHAPTER 1

1. *Political History of Jackson County* (Kansas City: Marshall and Morrison, 1902), p. 183; William Reddig, *Tom's Town, Kansas City and the Pendergast Legend* (New York: Lippincott, 1947), pp. 25, 29.
2. *Kansas City Star*, July 29, 1905.
3. United States Department of Interior, *Eleventh Census of the United States: 1890. Vital Statistics*, Vol. IV, Part II (Washington, D.C.: Government Printing Office, 1896), pp. 245–50. Wards 3 and 4 made up most of Quality Hill, and the Census shows that business houses were located there in many places by this time. Wards 8 and 9 were to the east of Quality Hill. Ward 9 was also south. Both wards had many good residences. Ward 8, the Census reported, encompassed the best residential neighborhood in the city.
4. *Kansas City Times*, March 20, 1888.
5. *Star*, March 15, 1892.
6. *Times*, March 26, 1892.
7. *Ibid.*

8. *Ibid.*
9. Kansas City, Missouri, *Charter of 1889* (Kansas City: Lawton, Hanens, and Burnap Stationers, 1889), Articles II, III.
10. Reddig, *op. cit.*, p. 38.
11. *Star*, March 15, 1893.
12. *Ibid.*, October 31, 1893; November 2, 1893.
13. *Ibid.*, August 24, 29, 1893.
14. Reddig, *op. cit.*, p. 29.
15. *Star*, December 11, 1893.
16. *Times*, January 30, 1894.
17. Charles P. Blackmore, "Joseph B. Shannon, Political Boss and Twentieth Century 'Jeffersonian' " (unpublished Ph.D. dissertation, Columbia University, 1954), pp. 8, 9, 38.
18. *Star*, March 14, 1894; April 9, 1894.
19. Quoted by Reddig, *op. cit.*, pp. 31–2.
20. *Star*, July 15, 1894.
22. *Ibid.*, November 8, 1895; January 10, 1896.
23. *Ibid.*, May 8, 1895.
24. *Ibid.*, December 9, 14, 1895.
25. *Ibid.*, February 22, 1896.
26. *Ibid.*, January 10, 1895.
27. *Ibid.*, December 27, 1894.
28. *Ibid.*, May 26, 1895.
29. *Kansas City Journal*, November 11, 1911.

CHAPTER 2
1. Reddig, *op. cit.*, p. 29.
2. *Star*, July 15, 1894; November 2, 1895.
3. *Ibid.*, January 2, 1896.
4. Blackmore, *op. cit.*, pp. 72–6.
5. Frank M. Lowe, Jr., *A Warrior Lawyer* (New York: Fleming H. Revell Company, 1942), pp. 68, 81–2; Blackmore *op. cit.*, p. 81.
6. *Star*, June 28, 1898.
7. *Ibid.*, July 24, 1898.
8. *Ibid.*
9. *Ibid.*, November 27, 28, 1893; May 3, 1894; July 24, 1898.
10. *Times*, November 11, 1911.
11. *Ibid.*
12. James W. S. Peters, "Home Rule Charter Movements in Missouri with Special Reference to Kansas City," *Annals of the American Academy of Political and Social Science*, XXVII (January 1906), p. 156.
13. *Kansas City World*, February 21, 1900.
14. *Ibid.*
15. *Star*, March 6, 29, 1900; *Journal*, April 3, 1900.

16. *Star,* March 9, 1900.
17. *Ibid.,* March 28, 1900.
18. *Ibid.,* April 3, 1900.
19. *Journal,* April 3, 1900.
20. Reddig, *op. cit.,* p. 71.
21. *Star,* April 4, 1900.
22. *Ibid.,* May 24, 1900.
23. *Journal,* July 26, 1902.
24. Blackmore, *op. cit.,* p. 137.
25. *The State ex rel. Yates et al. v. Crittenden County Clerk,* 164 Mo. 237 (1901).
26. *Star,* October 24, 1900.
27. *Ibid.,* January 30, 1902.
28. *Ibid.,* August 12, 1904.
29. *Journal,* July 26, 1902.
30. *Ibid.*
31. Peters, *op. cit.,* p. 161.
32. *World,* February 26, 1905.
33. *Ibid.,* February 27, 1905.
34. *Ibid.*
35. *Journal,* March 8, 1905.
36. A. Theodore Brown, *The Politics of Reform, Kansas City's Municipal Government, 1925–1950* (Kansas City: Community Studies, Inc., 1958), p. 20.
37. *Journal,* November 11, 1911.
38. Reddig, *op. cit.,* p. 71.

CHAPTER 3

1. *Star,* January 28, 1902.
2. Reddig, *op. cit.,* pp. 32–3.
3. George Creel, *Rebel at Large* (New York: G. P. Putnam's Sons, 1947), pp. 50–1.
4. Reddig, *op. cit.,* pp. 32–3.
5. An article appeared in the *Missouri Democrat* (Kansas City), October 21, 1927, which tells the story of the origin of the names "Goat" and "Rabbit" for the Pendergast and Shannon factions respectively. The term "Rabbit" caught on for the Shannon men soon after Joe Shannon casually commented on one occasion that he had rabbits on every corner, one night, prepared to inform him when they saw the governor arrive in town. Soon after that, one of Alderman Jim's cohorts suggested that the Pendergast faction needed a nickname. Jim Pendergast suggested "Goats" because he owned some, and because a lot of people in his First Ward, who lived on the West Bluffs, owned them too.
6. *The Rising Son* (Kansas City), October 25, 1906.

7. *Star*, December 2, 1907.
8. *World*, February 15, 1908.
9. *Ibid.*, February 27, 1908.
10. *Ibid.*, February 29, 1908.
11. *Star*, February 3, 1908.
12. *Journal*, October 31, 1914.
13. Quoted in Blackmore, *op. cit.*, p. 164.
14. Ewing Young Mitchell Papers (MSS Western Historical Manuscripts Collection, University of Missouri), Letter to E. Y. Mitchell from Ewing Bland, February 13, 1912, Box 15, fol. 522.

CHAPTER 4

1. Information on the padding in various wards can be found in the Herbert S. Hadley Papers (MSS Western Historical Manuscripts Collection, University of Missouri), Letter to Governor Hadley from J. M. Lowe, February 8, 1910, Box 5, fol. 96A.
2. Hadley Papers, Letter to Hadley from Homer Mann, September 27, 1910, Box 5, fol. 96A.
3. *Star*, March 10, 1912.
4. *Times*, April 3, 1912.
5. The ward boundaries changed between 1910 and 1912. Consequently, it is impossible to compare election returns from the wards to see just how much the ward organization helped the machine cause.
6. Reddig, *op. cit.*, p. 67.
7. William L. Riordon, ed., *Plunkitt of Tammany Hall* (New York: Alfred A. Knopf, 1948), p. xviii.
8. Reddig, *op. cit.*, p. 95.
9. *Examiner* (Independence, Missouri), August 3, 1914.
10. *Star*, August 7, 1912.
11. *Ibid.*
12. Ralph L. Lozier Papers (MSS Western Historical Manuscripts Collection, University of Missouri), Copy of letter from T. J. Pendergast to Woodrow Wilson, March 14, 1913.
13. Frank Walsh Papers (MSS New York Public Library), Letter to Jerome Walsh from Frank Walsh, February 20, 1932, Box 134.
14. *Star*, March 5, 1914.
15. *Ibid.*, September 4, 1929.
16. *Ibid.*, April 2, 1920.
17. Mitchell Papers, Letter to E. Y. Mitchell from Ewing Bland of Kansas City, September 28, 1916, Box 40, fol. 1448.
18. *Star*, July 3, 4, 1914.
19. *Ibid.*, July 8, 1914.
20. *Times*, July 8, 1914.
21. Francis M. Wilson Papers (MSS Western Historical Manuscripts

Collection, University of Missouri). Typed copies of the sworn affidavits and testimony given in circuit court in Kansas City during February and April 1915 contain much evidence to support these statements. The testimony runs to nearly 200 pages and can be found in Boxes 31 and 32, fols. 1006–20. The *Star*, July 8, 1914, reported that one repeat voter was sentenced to two years in prison less than a week after the election.

22. Wilson Papers, Court testimony and sworn affidavits, Boxes 31 and 32, fols. 1006–20.

CHAPTER 5

1. Reddig, *op. cit.*, pp. 109–15.
2. *Examiner*, July 30, 1914.
3. *Ibid.*, July 27, 1914.
4. *Star*, August 5, 1914.
5. *Examiner*, November 4, 1914; *Star*, August 11, 1914.
6. *Star*, March 16, 1916.
7. *Ibid.*, March 2, 1916.
8. *Ibid.*, March 14, 15, 1916.
9. *Labor Herald* (Kansas City), March 31, 1916.
10. *Star*, April 3, 1916.
11. *Ibid.*, April 4, 1916.
12. Blackmore, *op. cit.*, p. 168.
13. *Examiner*, November 8, 1916.
14. Mitchell Papers, Letters to E. Y. Mitchell from Ewing Bland, September 10 and 28, 1916, Box 40, fols. 1439 and 1448.
15. Donald B. Oster, "Kansas City, Missouri Charter Movements, 1905–1925" (unpublished M. A. thesis, University of Kansas City, 1962), pp. 123–4.
16. *Star*, November 3, 1918.
17. Mitchell Papers, Letter to E. Y. Mitchell from Ewing Bland, November 9, 1918, Box 50, fol. 1798. Throughout the campaign the *Star* attacked Bulger's record.
18. For examples of how Pendergast worked with the Republican party see letters in the Guy B. Park Papers (MSS Western Historical Manuscripts Collection, University of Missouri), Box 51, fol. 1671. Letter from Ray B. Horton to Park dated June 22, 1934, points out that he had worked with Pendergast for years. For the particular election under discussion here see the August 4, 1920, issue of the *Star*.
19. *Times*, April 7, 1920.
20. Robert P. Friedman, "The Public Speaking of Arthur M. Hyde" (unpublished Ph.D. dissertation, University of Missouri, 1954), pp. 169–70, 183–5.
21. Harry S Truman, *Year of Decisions*, Vol. I of *Memoirs by Harry*

S *Truman* (Garden City: Doubleday & Company, 1955), pp. 136–37; Jonathan Daniels, *The Man of Independence* (New York: J. B. Lippincott, 1950), pp. 109–13.

22. *Star*, December 28, 1922; Truman, *op. cit.*, pp. 137–8.
23. Reddig, *op. cit.*, p. 269; Truman also was appointed 2nd Vice-President of the Jackson Democratic Club, Inc., in May 1929. It was the parent club of all of the Pendergast ward and district clubs.
24. Eugene Francis Schmidtlein, "Truman the Senator" (unpublished Ph.D. dissertation, University of Missouri, 1962), pp. 35–7.
25. Walter Matscheck, *History of the Kansas City Civic Research Institute* (unpublished, 1963).
26. *Missouri Democrat*, November 10, 1933.
27. Truman informed Jonathan Daniels that John J. Pryor, William D. Boyle, and W. A. Ross were "the crooked contractors that caused the scandals under Bulger." See Daniels, *op. cit.*, p. 147.

CHAPTER 6

1. *Times*, April 7, 1920; *Star*, April 10, 1920.
2. Hyde Papers, Letter to Hyde from Frank Johnston, April 19, 1922, Box 32, fol. 738A.
3. Brown, *op. cit.*, pp. 31–2.
4. Quoted in Reddig, *op. cit.*, p. 116.
5. Oster, *op. cit.*, p. 206.
6. Brown, *op. cit.*, p. 34.
7. *Times*, October 1, 1925.
8. *Star*, November 1, 1925.
9. *Missouri Democrat*, November 6, 1925.
10. Lloyd C. Stark Papers (MSS Western Historical Manuscripts Collection, University of Missouri), Letter to Stark from Clarence Cannon, November 27, 1934, Box 304, fol. 7631 says that "Harry S. Jacks, the real owner of the Missouri Democrat . . . is an able man and in high favor with the powers that be in K. C."
11. Stark Papers, Letter to Stark from Clarence Cannon, February 18, 1935, Box 306, fol. 7667.
12. *Missouri Democrat*, August 26, 1927.
13. Stark Papers, Letter to Stark from Herbert M. Woolf, October 24, 1935, Box 315, fol. 7924.
14. Stark Papers, Letter to Stark from Reginald Frame, October 16, 1935, Box 309, fol. 7754.
15. Brown, *op. cit.*, p. 51.
16. *Missouri Democrat*, July 22, 1932.
17. Stark Papers, Box 490, fol. 12261.
18. *Star*, December 18, 1921.
19. Quoted by Carey James Tate, "Julia Lee," *The Second Line* (January 1960), p. 11.

20. Gordon Stevenson, *A Brief History of Jazz in Kansas City* (unpublished manuscript in the Missouri Valley Room, Kansas City, Missouri Public Library).
21. Tate, *op. cit.*, p. 10.
22. Fred Allhoff, "Thunder Over Kansas City," *Liberty* (September 17, 1938), p. 4.

CHAPTER 7

1. Even in St. Louis the Democrats fared poorly in the 1920's. In some of the national contests Democrats received more votes than their Republican opponents but in the city elections, Republicans had complete control. The Republicans dominated the mayoralty contests with Henry Kiel and Victor J. Miller. The G.O.P. consistently controlled the council as well.
2. Stark Papers, Letter to Stark from William Ledbetter, March 24, 1930, Box 300, fol. 7552.
3. *Missouri Democrat*, June 13, 1930.
4. Wilson Papers, August 8, 1931, Box 16, fol. 489.
5. *Ibid.*, Letter to Francis Wilson from C. M. Edwards, December 6, 1931, Box 15, fol. 469.
6. Stark Papers, Copy of a letter from Stark to Clarence Cannon, April 4, 1932, Box 301, fol. 7559.
7. *Ibid.*, Copy of letter from Stark to Clarence Cannon, April 4, 1932, and from Cannon to Stark, April 11, 1932, Box 301, fol. 7559.
8. Mitchell Papers, Letter from Ewing Cockrell to E. Y. Mitchell, July 22, 1932, Box 71, fol. 2498.
9. Jesse W. Barrett Papers (MSS Western Historical Manuscripts Collection, University of Missouri), Letter to Barrett from John Gillis November 23, 1931, Box 46, fol. 1282; Wilson Papers, Letter to Wilson from E. T. McGaugh, September 5, 1931, Box 24, fol. 790; Francis Wilson to William Hirth, undated (probably January 1932), Box 11, fol. 333.
10. Wilson Papers, Letter to Wilson from George G. Vest, February 18, 1932, Box 28, fol. 949.
11. *Ibid.*, Copy of letter from Wilson to Ray Cherry, January 22, 1928, Box 4, fol. 114 makes it clear that Igoe directed Wilson's campaign in St. Louis in 1928. He did so in 1932 after seeing Pendergast. See copy of the letter from Wilson to C. F. Newman, February 11, 1932, Box 28, fol. 941; copy of the letter from Wilson to Igoe, February 23, 1932, Box 29, fol. 956.
12. Stark Papers, Copy of letter from Stark to Dr. K. C. Sullivan, October 31, 1932, Box 303, fol. 7603.
13. Wilson Papers, Copy of letter from Wilson to William Hirth, undated (probably January 1932), Box 11, fol. 333.
14. Harry Hopkins Papers (MSS Franklin D. Roosevelt Library, Hyde

Park, New York), Letter to Hopkins from T. J. Edwards, February 9, 1934, Box 81, Missouri Reports.

15. Barrett Papers, Letter to Barrett from J. Gillis, February 13, 1932, Box 46, fol. 1286A.
16. *Ibid.*, Letter to Barrett from Frederick E. Whitten, March 2, 1936, Box 49, fol. 1399A.
17. Park Papers, Letter to Park from George Jones, June 2, 1933, Box 15, fol. 495; Letter to Park from Jim Pendergast, November 11, 1936, Box 52, fol. 1678; Letter to Park from Charles Orr, July 17, 1934, Box 51, fol. 1671; Letter to Park from Dr. Ray B. Horton, April 22, 1934, Box 51, fol. 1671; Barrett Papers, Letter to Barrett from William G. Lynch, July 29, 1936, Box 52, fol. 1492A.
18. Park Papers, Letter to Park from T. J. Pendergast, September 28, 1935, Box 52, fol. 1674.
19. *Ibid.*, Letter to Park with an accompanying photocopy of the petition from Dr. C. S. Cleveland of the Cleveland Chiropractic College in Kansas City, December 10, 1934, Box 52, fol. 1672.
20. *Ibid.*, Letter to Park from Hugh Pendergast, August 12, 1935, Box 52, fol. 1674.
21. Stark Papers, Box 490, fol. 12255.
22. Brown, *op. cit.*, pp. 66–9.
23. Elmer Irey and William Slocum, "How We Smashed the Pendergast Machine," *Coronet*, XXIII (December 1947), pp. 67–76.
24. Stark Papers, Letter to Stark from S. R. Toucey, July 29, 1937, Box 121, fol. 2720.
25. *Ibid.*, Letter to Stark from Howard Austin, November 13, 1936, Box 121, fol. 2712.
26. Park Papers, Letter from J. C. Nichols to Park, June 3, 1935, Box 27, fol. 873.
27. Barrett Papers, Letter to Barrett from Charles L. Dunham, April 14, 1938, Box 56, fol. 1696.

CHAPTER 8

1. Edwin O'Connor, *The Last Hurrah* (Boston: Little, Brown, 1956), p. 374.
2. A number of scholars assume that the New Deal destroyed the bosses, but they do not provide any evidence to support such an assumption. For example, the May 1964 issue of *The Annals* was devoted to the subject, "City Bosses and Political Machines." Most of the authors who contributed to that issue began with that assumption, but not one presented any concrete evidence.
3. This point of view is held by most Missourians today and it was expressed by the contemporary press. This is, in essence, the interpretation held by Reddig, *op. cit.*, pp. 204–5, 213. A notable ex-

ception to this interpretation is presented in Franklin Dean Mitchell, "Embattled Democracy: Missouri Democratic Politics, 1918–1932" (unpublished Ph.D. dissertation, University of Missouri, 1964).

4. Democratic National Committee, 1932 Correspondence (MSS Franklin D. Roosevelt Library, Hyde Park, New York), Letter to Roosevelt from Dunlap, July 9, 1931, 1928–33 file D.
5. *Missouri Democrat,* September 18, 1931.
6. Democratic National Committee Correspondence, Letter to Guernsey Cross from E. A. Green, March 30, 1932, Missouri Pre-Convention Box 324, file G.
7. *Ibid.,* Telegram from Ewing Young Mitchell to Roosevelt, March 30, 1932, Missouri Pre-Convention Box 325, file M.
8. *Ibid.,* Abstract of letter to Roosevelt from Dunlap, April 2, 1932, Missouri Pre-Convention Box 323, Abstract folder.
9. *Ibid.,* Letter to Roosevelt from Ike Dunlap, May 26, 1932, and May 31, 1932, Missouri Pre-Convention Box 324, file D.
10. *Ibid.*
11. Mitchell Papers, copy of letter from Mitchell to Emil Hurja, June 7, 1934, Box 83, fol. 2955.
12. Quoted in a letter from Bennett Clark to James A. Reed, cited by Frank Mitchell, *op. cit.,* p. 259.
13. *Ibid.,* pp. 259–60.
14. *Missouri Democrat,* July 10, 1932.
15. *Ibid.,* December 9, 1932.
16. Lozier Papers, Copy of letter to T. J. Pendergast from Ralph Lozier, April 17, 1933.
17. Reddig, *op. cit.,* pp. 182–3.
18. Mitchell Papers, Copy of letter from E. Y. Mitchell to Harry Hopkins, March 24, 1934, Box 82, fol. 2909.
19. Stark Papers, Letter to Stark from Jim Hurst, July 11, 1935, Box 309, fol. 7764.
20. Reddig, *op. cit.,* p. 271.
21. Mitchell Papers, Letter to Mitchell from G. H. Foree, June 19, 1934, Box 83, fol. 2963.
22. *Ibid.,* Letters to Mitchell from G. H. Foree, May 21, 1934, Box 83, fol. 2943; June 14, 1934, Box 83, fol. 2958; June 26, 1934, Box 84, fol. 2969.
23. *Missouri Democrat,* July 6, 1934.
24. Park Papers, Letter to Park from Orestes Mitchell, July 25, 1934, Box 66, fol. 2200. There is evidence in Box 15, fol. 504, that state employees were being assessed for Truman's campaign too.
25. Clipping dated July 12, 1934 in the Park Papers, Box 66, fol. 2200.
26. Reddig, *op. cit.,* p. 274.
27. Stark Papers, Letter to Stark from William Ledbetter, June 16, 1935, Box 309, fol. 7752.

28. Mitchell Papers, Letter to Mitchell from Haywood Scott, March 26, 1936, Box 90, fol. 3181.
29. Park Papers, Copy of letter from Park to Mrs. Hester B. Miller, June 21, 1935, Box 56, fol. 1825.
30. Barrett Papers, Photocopy of a letter from Truman to L. T. Slayton, February 5, 1935, Box 54, fol. 1566A.
31. Stark Papers, Letter to Stark from Jim Hurst, May 27, 1935, Box 308, fol. 7741.
32. Barrett Papers, Notorized affidavit, September 16, 1936, Box 53, fol. 1544. Stark himself received reports on how the WPA was used in his behalf. See, for example, Stark Papers, Letter to Stark from A. Moore, January 30, 1936, Box 319, fol. 8049.
33. Stark Papers, Letter to Stark from J. W. Hunolt, October 31, 1936, Box 348, fol. 8811.
34. Stark Papers, All files marked "Douglas Campaign," dated May to August 1938.

CHAPTER 9

1. Brown, *op. cit.*, p. 168.
2. *Ibid.*, pp. 177–8.
3. Stark Papers, Clipping from the *New York World*, July 12, 1935, Box 325, fol. 8220.
4. *Missouri Democrat*, September 9, 1933.
5. *Ibid.*, January 25, 1935.
6. Stark Papers, Copy of letter to Jim Hurst from Stark, May 1, 1935, Box 307, fol. 7714.
7. *Ibid.*, Letter to Mrs. Stark from Mrs. Amy Bradshaw, May 24, 1935.
8. *Ibid.*, Copy of letter from Stark to Clarence Cannon, February 25, 1935, Box 306, fol. 7671.
9. *Ibid.*, Letter to Stark from Jim Hurst, September 5, 1935, Box 312, fol. 7853.
10. *Ibid.*, Copy of letter to Jim Hurst from Stark, October 5, 1935, Box 313, fol. 7885; May 1, 1935, Box 307, fol. 7714.
11. *Ibid.*, see materials in Box 347, fol. 8784; and the copy of the letter from Stark to T. J. Pendergast, September 26, 1935, Box 313, fol. 7879.
12. Reddig, *op. cit.*, pp. 241–2.
13. Park Papers, Box 33, fol. 1060–62.
14. Brown, *op. cit.*, pp. 57–8, 415.
15. Reddig, *op. cit.*, p. 247.
16. Quoted, *ibid.*, p. 288.
17. Stark Papers, Letter to Stark from Mrs. McDaniel, September 15, 1938, Box 179, fol. 4010.
18. *Missouri Democrat*, April 8, 1938.
19. Stark Papers, Box 20, fol. 598; Box 21, fol. 622; Box 43, fol. 1099.

20. *Ibid.*, Letter to Stark from John Harding, May 5, 1939, Box 151, fol. 3417.
21. *Report of the Chief of Police Covering Reorganization Activities, and Accomplishments of the Kansas City, Mo., Police Department for the Calendar Year 1940* (December 1940).
22. The source of information here and in the next few paragraphs on Lazia and the gangsters in Kansas City is Reddig, *op. cit.*, pp. 248–64, 321–2; *Kansas City Star*, July 10, 11, 1934.
23. Stark Papers, Box 417, fol. 10788, contains twenty-nine letters written in March 1939 to J. L. Freeman, a member of the Missouri House of Representatives.
24. Irey and Slocum, *op. cit.*, p. 69.
25. Stark Papers, Box 179, fol. 4036.
26. *Ibid.* See copy of letter from Stark to Robert Hannegan, July 11, 1938, Box 180, fol. 4073; letters in Box 181, fols. 4083 and 4095; letter to Stark from J. Dorsey, July 6, 1938, Box 180, fol. 4068; clipping in Box 400, fol. 10351; Governor's orders, July 25, 1938, Box 183, fol. 4137.
27. *Ibid.*, Letter to Stark from B. M. Marshall, July 26, 1938, Box 183, fol. 4150.
28. *Ibid.*, See letters to Stark in Box 179, fols. 4033, 4044, 4054–5, and Box 180, fols. 4057, 4062, 4067–8.
29. Franklin D. Roosevelt Official File 300 (MSS Franklin D. Roosevelt Library, Hyde Park, New York), Copy of memo to Harry Hopkins from M. H. McIntyre summarizing telegram from Lloyd Stark, July 7, 1938, Box 41.
30. *Ibid.*, Telegram to Roosevelt from Stark, July 13, 1938.
31. James A. Farley, *Jim Farley's Story: The Roosevelt Years* (New York: McGraw-Hill Book Company, 1948), p. 134.
32. *Ibid.*, p. 108.
33. The evidence in the case against Pendergast is presented in Maurice Milligan, "Statement of facts to the Court in the case of U.S. vs. T. J. Pendergast, No. 14567." A copy of this statement is in the Western Historical Manuscripts Collection, University of Missouri. The eight companies listed as sources of Pendergast's income were Ready-Mixed Concrete Company, Midwest Asphalt Company, Midwest Paving Company, W. A. Ross Construction Company, Sanitary Service Company, Glendale Sales Company, Midwest PreCote Company, and Kansas City Concrete Pipe Company.
34. Reddig, *op. cit.*, pp. 327–8.
35. *Ibid.*, pp. 335–6.
36. Harry S Truman Papers (MSS Harry S Truman Library, Independence, Missouri), Copy of letter to A. V. Burrowes from Truman January 8, 1944, Senatorial files.

37. *Ibid.*, Letter to Truman from Bryce Smith, October 22, 1943, Senatorial files. The "Star" referred to in the quotation is the newspaper, the *Kansas City Star.*

38. *Ibid.*, Copy of letter to John T. Barlow from Truman, May 26, 1941, Senatorial files.

39. *Ibid.*, Copy of letter to Walter H. Williams from Truman, November 28, 1942, Senatorial files.

Bibliographic Essay

Most of the books and articles written about the Pendergast machine and Kansas City are inaccurate polemics charged with emotion. An outstanding exception is William Reddig, *Tom's Town: Kansas City and the Pendergast Legend* (New York, 1947). Reddig's journalistic account of Kansas City during the Pendergast era is a well-written book based on newspaper articles and the author's personal acquaintance with Kansas City during part of those years. The first serious scholar to work on politics in Kansas City was A. Theodore Brown. His excellent book, *The Politics of Reform: Kansas City's Municipal Government, 1925–1950* (Kansas City, 1958), is a model study of local government. Covering the first twenty-five years of the city government under the council-manager charter, this book clearly describes how the machine managed the city. Aside from these books though, nothing of merit has been done on the Pendergast machine.

Perhaps scholars have been discouraged from writing a history of the Pendergast machine because no collection of Pendergast papers exists. This gap in source material forced me to rely heavily upon local newspapers for the early years of the machine. This paucity of manuscripts is not as serious a problem for the years after Jim Pendergast's death. Many of Tom Pendergast's letters are in the Western Historical Manuscripts Collection at the State Historical Society of Missouri, Columbia, Missouri. Likewise, the Western Historical Manuscripts Collection houses the papers of many leading Missouri politicians. Fourteen manuscript collections contained letters to and from Pendergast and his lieutenants, and many of these collections were rich with other letters relating to the Pendergast machine. Especially useful were the papers of Governors Lloyd C. Stark and Guy B. Park. Also, the papers of Jesse W. Barrett, Francis M. Wilson, Ewing Young Mitchell, and Ralph Lozier were valuable.

The Franklin D. Roosevelt Library at Hyde Park, New York, was indispensable. The papers of the Democratic National Committee for Missouri yielded material describing the local political scene. The Harry Hopkins Papers contain materials which demonstrate how Pendergast used Federal relief programs to his advantage; and Franklin D. Roosevelt's Official Files also hold significant material. The Frank Walsh Papers in the New York Public Library provide information about Federal patronage and the Pendergast machine.

The Board of Election Commissioners has no records of elections for the period of this study, but this presents no problem. The newspapers and the volumes of the *Official Manual* for Missouri contain all of the election returns. The State Historical Society of Missouri houses all of the volumes of the *Official Manual,* as well as complete or nearly complete files of most Missouri newspapers.

Extremely useful were my personal interviews with James M. Pendergast, the nephew of Alderman Jim and Tom Pendergast. Also helpful were interviews with Governor Lloyd C. Stark and with Walter Matscheck, who directed the Kansas City Civic Research Institute.

Anyone interested in a more fully documented version of this study should consult my unpublished Ph.D. dissertation, "A History of the Pendergast Machine" (University of Missouri, 1965).

Index

American Federation of Labor, 66
American Legion, 71
American Protective Association, 15, 19
Atterbury, John C., 109
Austin, Howard, 99
Aylward, James, joins Pendergast faction, 73; strengthens Tom Pendergast, 74; supports new charter, 78–79; chairman of Jackson County Democratic party, 83; in charge of organization, 83; uses patronage to build organization, 87; entertains James Farley, 104; refuses opportunity to run for Senate, 112; directs Truman's 1934 campaign, 114; distrusts Lloyd Stark, 120

Bailey, Harvey, 127
Baltimore Hotel, 34
Banks, Paul, 88
Baptist Church, 71
Barker, S. A., 80
Barrett, Jesse, 121
Baseball, as a political club activity, 82

Basie, Count, 88
Baughman, Booth, 68
Beach, Albert I., supports new charter, 77; runs for mayor under new charter, 79; re-elected mayor, 80
Becker, Charles, 97
Bell, C. Jasper, 80
Benanti, Frank, 126
Berlau Paper Company, 128
Billings, James V., 130
Bivona, Anthony, 126
Blitz, "Pinky," 25
Board of Election Commissioners, 80, 124
Board of Police Commissioners, 34, 64
Borden's Dairy, 128
"Boss Republicans," *see* Tom Marks
"Bossism," issue in 1932 campaign, 93
Bowling, as a political club activity, 83
Bradshaw, James T., 83
Brown, A. Theodore, quoted, 40, 79, 118
Brown, Marcy K., a power in county